In Faulkner's Shadow

In Faulkner's Shadow

A Memoir

LAWRENCE WELLS

University Press of Mississippi
Jackson

Willie Morris Books in Memoir and Biography

The University Press of Mississippi is the scholarly publishing agency of the Mississippi Institutions of Higher Learning: Alcorn State University, Delta State University, Jackson State University, Mississippi State University, Mississippi University for Women, Mississippi Valley State University, University of Mississippi, and University of Southern Mississippi.

www.upress.state.ms.us

Designed by Peter D. Halverson

The University Press of Mississippi is a member of the Association of University Presses.

Manufactured in the United States of America

First printing 2020

∞

Library of Congress Cataloging-in-Publication Data available

Hardback ISBN 978-1-4968-2991-7
Epub single ISBN 978-1-4968-2993-1
Epub institutional ISBN 978-1-4968-2994-8
PDF single ISBN 978-1-4968-2995-5
PDF institutional 978-1-4968-2996-2

British Library Cataloging-in-Publication Data available

With love and admiration to Diane, Paige, Jon,
Lawrence, and Catherine,
and in loving memory of Dean and Louise

We live in an old chaos of the sun
Or old dependency of day and night
—Wallace Stevens

Contents

In Faulkner's Shadow

Prologue

Across Time

A five-knot breeze stirred the oak trees beside the Lafayette County courthouse. Word had spread that Oxford would salute America's 200th birthday with a balloon ascension. By eight-thirty a.m. people began to assemble in twos and threes. Children on bicycles circled the square. Seated on the courthouse steps was a dark-haired young woman dressed in a striped T-shirt and jeans. She was my wife, Dean Faulkner Wells, daughter and namesake of William Faulkner's youngest brother. As publicity coordinator for the Fourth of July bicentennial in Oxford, Mississippi, I was charged with organizing the balloon event. My assignment was to draw a crowd to the square and keep them there for the speechmaking. As we waited for the balloonists to arrive Dean told me about a 1905 balloon ascension on the square. Her uncle Murry C. "Jack" Falkner, younger brother of William, was there. I have taken the liberty to paraphrase his recollections:

The crew, a tall, gangling black man and a surly, unshaven white man, arrive without ceremony on the square, hitch their wagon, and haul out a dirty, folded canvas canopy, ropes, stakes, and cordwood. Onlookers begin to gather as the black man selects a spot in the center of the unpaved street that circles the courthouse. After he digs a fire pit, he begins to lay a fire. The white man, likewise, makes his preparations. He gets out a jug of corn whiskey and begins to drink.

A rainbow-hued Volkswagen van marked "Hot Air, Inc." circled the courthouse twice before stopping. Dean and I welcomed balloon pilot Lin Stanton of Greenwood and his brother, Mark. Dean mentioned that this was her first lighter-than-air flight, and Stanton asked if she had any reservations. "No, why should I," she said. It wasn't a question.

"Well, sometimes," said Stanton, somewhat taken aback, "I've seen women panic."

"I wouldn't say that too loud if I were you," said Dean. "Some of my best friends are women."

He changed the subject. "Is anyone else going?"

"My husband. I'll vouch for him."

In their house two blocks from the square the Falkner boys—William, eight, Jack, six, John, four—slip out the kitchen door, escaping their mother's watchful eye, and hurry to town. Their adventurous spirit is rewarded by the sight of an enormous grayish-black canvas bag being laid out and attached by ropes to stakes set in a circle. In the center a fire burns briskly. The Falkner boys watch the black man pour coal oil on the fire and the white man drink from the jug balanced on his shoulder. Most of the thick black smoke blows into the eyes and throats of the spectators, though some of it causes gentle billows within the huge bag.

Dean and I helped distribute American flags and shooed curious children away from the balloonists. This was the second marriage for each of us, and after four years it was proving successful. We had received our graduate degrees and were teaching at a community college. Family time revolved around meals, school, homework, the children's activities, and three loads of laundry per day. Every week we attended a junior high basketball game, school play, or church supper. If Dean was hoping I'd whisk her to New Orleans, she was out of luck. All I could offer was a balloon ride.

"Hey, lady," I told my wife. "Want to fly away with me?"

Stanton, who was also a crop-duster pilot and ex-paratrooper, informed us that he'd filed a flight plan for a 9:30 takeoff. He and his brother unloaded the gondola and began to inflate the

77,500-cubic-foot, hot-air balloon, "Miss Cotton," seventy feet long and made of rip-stop nylon decorated in black, yellow, green, red, and white. The Stantons attached an aluminum frame and strapped into place two liquid-propane tanks. Their flight equipment included a temperature gauge, altimeter, compass, and rate-of-climb indicator. People of all ages pressed forward to see inside the gondola.

By noon, horses and mules have been removed from the square, partly to protect them from the blinding smoke and partly to make room for an increasing number of excited spectators to whom the choking, sooty smoke is an acceptable risk. The Falkner brothers, like the rest, are covered with greasy soot. Their faces are streaked with tears. They have never been so happy. The fire is roaring but the balloon is only half-inflated. Smoke spews through holes in the ancient fabric, and the black man, intermittently visible through dense billows of smoke, goes about calmly sealing the breaks with clothespins. Hidden in the smoke, the Falkner boys hear their nurse Caroline Barr calling them and realize that she has orders to find them and bring them home. They remain where the smoke is the thickest, keep quiet, and watch the pilot sitting on a keg. He drinks from his crock while watching the greasy smoke unfurling from beneath the canvas.

Stanton cranked a motorized fan, blew unheated air into the balloon, and like an elephant shaking off sleep Miss Cotton stirred and sat up. The spectators moaned in anticipation. Dean's three children, Diane, Paige, and Jon, arrived on the square with their grandmother, Louise. Stanton disappeared inside the balloon. Jon stared into the red recesses of the canopy. "Can I go in?" he asked. "Not right now," said his mother.

After tying canopy-release sashes to the tabs Stanton ordered, "Y'all get back! I'm going to heat her up!" Easing into the gondola resting on its side Stanton pulled the blast valve lever sending a twenty-foot flame roaring into Miss Cotton. The canopy ceased lolling about and expanded. Onlookers fell silent as Miss Cotton rose into the air. A sudden gust tilted the four-stories-high balloon. Spectators leapt out of the way. Police officers steadied the gondola. Stanton gave the valve another short blast, and the balloon righted itself.

Some of the smoke swirling in voluminous clouds around the canvas balloon has actually gotten inside it, and soon it begins to sway and tug at the restraining ropes. The pilot's assistant attaches a large, flat "basket" to the balloon with four ropes. He gently persuades the pilot to get aboard with his crock. In the process the basket dips too close to the fire, and one rope is burnt in two. The basket cants precariously to one side, with the pilot lying on his back, holding on with one hand and drinking from his crock with the other. The balloon strains at its ropes; the Falkner boys are rigid with anticipation. The pilot puts his jug down long enough to yell, "Cut, dammit, cut!"

We'd been expecting Mayor John Leslie to ride in the balloon, but so far he hadn't shown up. Stanton was worried about lifting off in an 80-plus degree temperature. In order to achieve lift, Stanton explained, the air inside the canopy needed to be 140 degrees hotter than the outside air.

"We can't delay any longer," he said.

"What do you want us to do?" asked Dean.

"Get in and hold on!" Stanton said, and so we did. Sweating from the heat of the burner he pulled on a crumpled flying cap adorned with 82nd Airborne paratrooper wings. His expression, youthful and intent a scant half-hour ago, was now focused and purposeful. All around us electronic cameras whirred with machinegun-like bursts. Young children, including Dean's son, raised a keening cry. The balloon leaned under a gust, dragging policemen with it.

The pilot's assistant whirls into action. Through the dense billows of smoke, the Falkner brothers can see him dashing feverishly from rope to rope. They hear the "thunk" of his ax. Their heads tilt back at the sight of the balloon miraculously rising. They hear the pilot cursing the canting basket. Borne on a gentle breeze from the north, the craft barely clears the buildings on the south end of the square. The three brothers exchange an electric stare of recognition. The balloon is headed straight toward their home.

"Ease up, give her some slack," ordered Mark Stanton. One of policemen let go of the rope, and the balloon turned a half-revolution. "*Let go!*" Stanton accented his command with a blast of flame. The officers fell back, and freed from restraint Miss Cotton began to ascend at a rate of twenty feet per second. Every face turned upward. Hands waved American flags. Another blast from Stanton and the gondola cleared City Hall by two feet. Diminishing behind us was the nineteenth-century courthouse, which William Faulkner called "the hub, the center." Streets stretched away from the square in orderly fashion. Rooftops and tree-lined boulevards revealed themselves. "East-northeast at eight knots!" Stanton sang.

The sun was in our faces, the wind at our backs. Except for periodic jets of flame there was no sound. We floated over St. Peter's Cemetery where my wife's father, Dean Swift Faulkner, a pilot killed four months before she was born, lay buried under the biblical inscription *I bare him on eagles' wings and brought him unto me*. The balloon's shadow crossed over the high-school athletic field darkening the upturned faces of sprinters.

"How do you like it?" Stanton said.

The Falkner boys race south after the low-flying balloon, which leaves a gray trail of black oily smoke seeping through holes in the canvas. With William in the lead, they leap around the corner of Brown's Commissary and take a shortcut through lots and gullies behind the buildings. They are gaining on the slow-flying balloon but find it dangerous to keep their eyes on the sky while running pell-mell over uneven terrain. Skinned shins and all, they gain on the balloon. The pilot, hanging on to the canted basket with one hand, talks to them between swigs at his crock. Being out of breath, they are unable to join in the conversation.

"Balloon truck, this is the balloon. Do you read me?" said Stanton, establishing contact with Mark, who was following in the Volkswagen van. Miss Cotton sailed over a subdivision near Campground Road. "See the treetops swirling in the distance?" Stanton observed. "That's a thermal. Like a dust devil, it can take you up five thousand feet before it lets go."

The gondola brushed the tips of fifty-foot-tall longleaf pines. Dean reached out and touched green needles. The hills rolled beneath us like ocean swells. Below, children chased the balloon, jumping up and down in Miss Cotton's shadow. "Where y'all going?" shouted a little girl.

"Montgomery!" Stanton called to her. "Is this the right way?"

A fence blocks the boys' way. While climbing over it they temporarily lose sight of the balloon. William and Jack pause to haul four-year-old John over the fence by the seat of his pants, then all three race at top speed as the balloon descends miraculously into their own backyard. They cannot believe their good fortune.

Floating with the wind made us feel as if we weren't moving even though our eyes told us differently. Then the wind shifted and we drifted southeast toward Highway 6. Mark reported his position on Highway 30. Lin advised him to take a right on Campground Road, then left on Highway 6. "Flying in the Delta has spoiled me," Stanton observed. "It's so flat you can land in any cotton field, but don't worry, we'll find a place to set down."

"I don't care if we go all the way to Tupelo," said Dean.

In the Falkner backyard three pet ponies graze on the lawn. Chickens cluck in the henhouse. The boys' mother, Maud Butler Falkner, tends the clothesline, while their nurse, Caroline, reports that she could not find the boys on the square. The faces of mother, nurse, and ponies turn upward as the balloon drifts over the yard. The pilot waves his crock at them, the balloon on the way down. With an oily sigh, it settles on top of the henhouse and wearily collapses.

A strip of pasture came into view but the closer we came, the smaller the field looked. To land there seemed like threading a needle, yet having made up his mind Stanton released hot air and began the descent. At the sight of the balloon a small herd of cattle stampeded, looking as lean and nimble as gazelles. Stanton blasted enough flame to clear a treetop, then yanked the sash to release hot air. Miss Cotton lost twenty feet of altitude before a gust of wind forced the gondola into a tall pine. Dean laughed as she brushed pine needles out of her hair. Stanton said, "Hold on, bend your knees and brace yourself. If we tilt over, hang onto the railing. Don't jump out before the gondola stops moving."

The pasture rose to meet us. A crosswind nudged the balloon into a wide ravine. "Hang on," said Stanton, unnecessarily. The gondola splashed into a stream and thumped into the far side of the ravine. We held on tight as the half-inflated balloon dragged us across the pasture. At last the bright-colored canopy collapsed over a dead tree with the gondola leaning against a barbed-wire fence.

The Falkner brothers hurry to the henhouse and slide to a halt. The pilot is rolling across the roof, holding his crock protectively high. Shingles scatter under his feet. The ponies back away, stamping their hooves. Mother and nurse are not impressed.

"This man may be hurt," says Maud Falkner, drawing herself up to her full four feet, eight inches. Equally determined, "Mammy Callie" Barr is not in a mood to sympathize. "If he ain't, he's going to be!" She seizes a piece of scantling and rushes at the sky-borne invader. Before coming within striking range, she catches sight of her charges, the breathless, astonished brothers, their once-clean clothes covered with soot, elbows scratched and bleeding. The pilot uses this distraction to slide off the roof and escape. Ragged, dirty, and exhilarated, the three brothers stand before their mother to receive judgment.

The gondola rested on its side. Dean and I crawled out gingerly, reluctant to return to earth. Balloon flight was not unlike reading one of her uncle William's short stories, where one is released from the ordinary, trusts in his pilot and becomes one with the wind. From my time with Dean I had observed that the Faulkner heritage was an uneasy legacy. There were times when she embraced her roots and her famous uncle. At other times she felt trapped and stultified. Where did *she* begin and *it* end? Her famous uncle had solved this riddle long ago. "The past is never dead," Faulkner wrote. "It's not even past."

1. Faulkner Family

- 1 -

What's a Participle?

We met at the University of Mississippi in a Beowulf seminar. Professor Louis Dollarhide began to lecture as he entered the classroom. The compound *berserk*, he said, meant bare of one's "sark," the ring-mail shirt worn into battle. The fiercest of the Danes would rip off his protective armor and race bare-sark into battle. "This often proved fatal," Dollarhide added. I risked a glance at the young woman who sat across the table from me. Word was out that Faulkner's niece, recently divorced, had enrolled in graduate school. A fellow student pointed her out to me before class. She was named for her father, Dean Swift Faulkner, a professional pilot killed in the biplane his brother William had given him. Her uncle William, or "Pappy" as she knew him, became her legal guardian and paid for her schooling. Instead of taking notes Dean seemed to listen to a clash of Viking swords, head slightly tilted, dark hair framing her face.

Prior to enrolling at the University of Mississippi I taught English for four years at Murray State University in Kentucky. An Ole Miss professor came to Murray on a recruiting trip and convinced me to apply to Ole Miss's fledgling PhD program in English. As I drove to Oxford on the winding Highway 7 past hardscrabble farms and barren hills I felt that I was entering Flem Snopes country. A few minutes later I entered the oak-lined streets north of Oxford's square, antebellum homes and caught sight of the courthouse framed by towering oaks. I had arrived in the other half of Faulkner's fictional cosmos, the town of Jefferson. "It's true!" I thought. "Faulkner didn't make it up."

Oxford in 1970 was a small college town of ten thousand permanent residents. The university's eight thousand students lived mostly on campus and avoided establishments frequented by "adults." Eight years after James Meredith enrolled at Ole Miss the integration of the university was very much a work in progress. That fall the Ole Miss football team would field its first African American player, Ben Williams, a freshman nose-tackle from Yazoo City. Vietnam vets of every race and religion walked to class sporting fatigue jackets and shoulder-length hair. Ole Miss was flower-child territory. There were rock concerts in the Grove—the wooded tailgating area at the center of the campus—and clouds of marijuana smoke. University police sporting long sideburns looked the other way. Woodstock had come to Mississippi.

My wife, Gayle, and I rented a two-bedroom basement apartment on South Lamar Boulevard and settled in with our two children, Lawrence, five years old, and Catherine, eighteen months. Our neighbors across the street were Mac Reed, co-owner of Gathright Reed pharmacy and a friend of William Faulkner. Mac and his wife invited Gayle and me for coffee, and he reminisced about packing Faulkner's manuscripts in the 1940s and mailing them off to publishers.

But the author's portrayal of slavery and reconstruction did not set well with most white Mississippians, many of whom denigrated the writer and disparaged his work sight unseen. I soon blundered into the prejudice that had plagued Oxford's most famous native all his life.

When the ancient Royal standard typewriter that I inherited from my grandfather broke down, I took it to Varner's Repair Shop on the square. Mr. Varner had lost his arm in an accident yet could fix anything with one hand. He examined my broken typewriter and began writing a receipt. I couldn't resist remarking that Faulkner had used the name "Varner" in *The Hamlet* and that in the novel Will Varner owned the general store in Frenchman's Bend. The repairman didn't look up. I added that Faulkner made Will Varner the richest man in the county.

"If that Faulkner feller was still around," Varner muttered, "I wouldn't cross the street to speak to him."

The Beowulf seminar had been over for an hour when I ran into Dean in the corridor.

"*What's a participle?*" Her first words to me could have come from those fabled matchmakers, grammarians Strunk and White. We were standing in the lobby of Bondurant Hall. Classes were changing, students filling the hallway. She was about five foot four, tiny waisted, and slender.

"Let me guess," I said. "A student asked you to define *participle*?"

She nodded. "It's been an ice age since I thought about grammar and usage."

Most people raise their voices to be heard. Dean whispered and listeners leaned in.

I leaned in. "Excuse me?"

"Please, if you don't mind, what is a participle?"

"The *-ing* form of a verb, as in running."

"Of course, how stupid of me!" She stuck out her hand to introduce herself. "I'm Dean Mallard," she said, using her married name. "An hour before classes started," she went on, "Dr. Webb [the chairman of the English department] assigned me a freshman class to teach. I didn't have time to prepare. I've never taught anything except swimming lessons."

On impulse I asked if she'd like a cup of coffee, and to my astonishment she accepted.

"I noticed you in Beowulf class," she told me as we sat over coffee at the student union. It made me a little berserk to look at her, but being married I kept my shirt on. "You have blue eyes," she said. "I always wanted blue eyes. All of my family have them except for me, Nannie, and two uncles."

I thought of William Faulkner's dark eyes peering out of a famous Cofield photograph. So *that's* what she had seen in me?

I took Dean to my cubbyhole of an office and offered her my freshman composition syllabus, sample themes, and tests. All the teaching assistants except Dean had this material.

"Now go teach that hotshot who asked you what a participle is," I said.

She was delighted and within a few weeks was teaching composition as if she'd been doing it all her life. She soon became one of the most popular instructors in the Ole Miss English department. For the next five years until she received her master's degree, she instilled confidence and writing skills in hundreds of freshmen. Several law students audited her class.

We lived three blocks from each other on South Lamar Boulevard, the main thoroughfare. Dean had moved with her three children into her grandmother Maud Butler Falkner's house where she'd lived off and on. Our sons attended the same kindergarten, and we began to carpool. We attended the same graduate student gatherings and took our children to the movies together. Gayle even painted a portrait of Dean's kids which Dean cherished.

Not long after the fall semester began I discovered a telephone bill listing calls to Kentucky. I recognized the number. Apparently Gayle had become involved in a long-distance relationship with a twenty-one-year-old man, six years her junior. As a matter of fact, he still lived with his parents. The liaison appeared platonic, yet I demanded that she break it off. I was trying to make a better life for us. My goal was a tenure appointment at a university, perhaps at the University of Alabama where we both earned undergraduate degrees.

We began a war of words which led to accusations, barter, and eventually negotiations. Though we took pains not to fight in the presence of the children Lawrence knew something was wrong. He was sleeping poorly and talking to himself. Catherine by virtue of her young age was spared. Meanwhile, the marriage dissolved in whispers.

Dean became my confidante and advisor. "Get out of the house," she said. "Go to parties, see people!"

I honestly never imagined Dean and me as anything more than a friend and colleague. I never even fantasized about her. I was the father of two young children, and for their sake I wanted my marriage to survive. Over the coming months I asked myself if I'd ignored the long-distance telephone calls perhaps the flirtation would have faded from lack of resistance. What faded instead was our marriage. In August 1971, Gayle and I were divorced. Dean and I began dating in September.

Two years after Dean's death in 2011 her childhood friend, Sandra Baker Moore, shared a secret with me. On the day that Dean and I met, the *day-of-the-participle*, she phoned Sandra and said, "I've just met the man I want to spend the rest of my life with."

- 2 -

Legacy

Gayle and the children went to live in Birmingham with her parents. After Christmas she moved to Kentucky and married the young man at the other end of the telephone line. I wished only the best for her, but I missed my children terribly. Such is the brutal aftermath of divorce.

I believed fate brought Dean and me together but as far as she was concerned our meeting was a combination of fate *and* luck. A couple of times over the years, glancing at me in a thoughtful way, she remarked, "You remind me of Pappy."

Dean herself bore a stunning resemblance to her uncle. They both had dark hair, brown eyes, and a deliberate manner. She was soft-spoken yet with an air of total assurance. Faces brightened when she entered a room. People felt that they were in William's presence. When Faulkner's mistresses Meta Carpenter Wilde, Jean Stein, and Joan Williams met Dean on separate occasions, each burst into tears and gripped her hands. Perhaps they even saw in Dean the child they might have had with Bill.

It helped that she did not judge them. That they made her uncle happy was all that mattered to her.

We began the eternal process of getting to know each other's past. One night at the kitchen table I asked what it was like to grow up at Rowan Oak. She didn't like being asked. It was as if her memories were too dear to part with.

"Every Halloween," she told me, "Pappy would light a candle and tell ghost stories. He made up a poltergeist named Judith, the daughter of Colonel Sheegog, original owner of Rowan Oak. In Pappy's story, Judith committed suicide by jumping off the balcony. We never tired of hearing the story. Pappy would tell the bravest among us to carry the candle to Judith's grave. If the flame went out, he said, we could be sure Judith blew it out. Holding our breath we walked on tiptoe to the magnolia under which Judith was allegedly buried. When the flame went out, as it always did, we looked to Pappy for reassurance. Of course he'd slipped away and was nowhere to be seen."

"What did you do then?"

"Ran like hell. Every man for himself."

Maud Falkner was a huge influence in Dean's life. She called her granddaughter "Lamb," told her bedtime stories, and painted bucolic scenes on the bottom of her milk glass. To see the picture she had to finish her milk. Yet as with most of her Faulkner relatives Dean came to love "Nannie" not because of her virtues but in spite of her faults.

Miss Maud was a Spartan personality with a skeptical nature and a tendency to hold a grudge. She was proud of William's writings and compulsively defended him against his critics.

One day I noticed stacks of old *Time* magazines in the attic. When I asked about them Dean smiled, saying, "Nannie loved *Time* and kept her old issues, but when the magazine published an article about Pappy getting off a plane drunk, she canceled her subscription."

When Faulkner's sensationalistic novel *Sanctuary* was published in 1931, he was quoted as saying it was "deliberately conceived to make money." Maud's friends were more than eager to know if Faulkner had based the character "Temple Drake" on a certain judge's daughter, an Ole Miss coed and flapper in the Roaring Twenties. At a game of bridge one afternoon, one of the ladies summoned the nerve to ask, "Maud, why did Billy write that book?" Miss Maud lowered her cards. "My Billy writes what he has to," she replied, biting off each word. She finished playing the rubber and—this according to Dean, who'd heard the account from eyewitnesses—never played bridge with that foursome again.

Maud's disapproval could be formidable. She adored her four sons but not their wives—with the possible exception of Dean's mother, Louise. Known to friends as "MoWese" she had been widowed at twenty-two when her husband died in the plane crash. She lived with her mother-in-law until Dean was born.

When Dean was a teenager, her aunt Lucille, who was John Faulkner's wife, paid a call at Thanksgiving. She'd baked a cake for her mother-in-law. Delighted to see her aunt, Dean called her grandmother to the door. Maud held out her hands as if to take the cake, but when Lucille presented the cake box she dropped her hands. The cake fell to the floor and broke into pieces. Lucille stood shocked and incredulous. Maud told Dean, "Lamb, throw out the cake. It may be poisoned." Lucille fled in despair.

Dean never learned what caused her grandmother's grievance. Maud's maxim, "Don't Complain, Don't Explain," and its implied "Don't Apologize," caused unintended and hurtful separations.

Though ashamed of her grandmother's behavior on that occasion, Dean refused to take sides. At the same time, she was determined not to become the miniature Maud that her grandmother thought she was bringing up. Maud's motto was "Don't expect anything good to happen and you will never be disappointed." Dean's buoyant nature ran counter to such skepticism. Like her outgoing father she took life one day at a time. As an undergraduate she played tennis and swam freestyle. She inherited her father's love of sports and William's love of the written word.

At age thirteen she devoured Faulkner's novel *Intruder in the Dust* the night before attending the 1949 movie premiere. This was her first real awareness of her uncle's fame. In Oxford's Lyric Theatre she experienced the glare of celebrity with William, his wife, Estelle, and their daughter, Jill.

But it was seven years later that she became fully aware of her uncle's influence and reach. At twenty she was sailing to France to study abroad. William, who was paying for it, flew to New York to see her off. The night before she was to sail, "Pappy" and Random House editor Saxe Commins took her to dinner. She noticed heads turning as they walked down Park Avenue to her uncle's favorite restaurant. She felt certain they were staring at her, dressed in her black cotton sheath, her hair cut like her idol Françoise Sagan. But they were all staring at her uncle. That was the day she realized just how famous Pappy really was. This wasn't Oxford, Mississippi, where everyone knew his name, but New York City with total strangers gawking at the author.

My introduction to her uncle's work came rather late for an English major. I put off reading Faulkner until I was a senior at the University of Alabama. I began with *The Portable Faulkner*, Malcolm Cowley's explication of the "Yoknapatawpha saga." When the anthology first appeared in 1946, most of William Faulkner's books were out of print. Due in part to Cowley's masterful analysis Faulkner's achievement became more widely appreciated and he was awarded the 1949 Nobel Prize in Literature.

At first glance I recognized Faulkner's characters. Every town had a Flem Snopes. In my hometown of Ozark, Alabama, I remembered a wealthy loner whose hobby was collecting coke bottles for the deposits. In the doomed Sartorises I saw my Wells grandfather, vice president of a bank that failed during the Depression. The McCaslins were close kin to the McGees, my mother's Scotch-Irish clan, gregarious and proud. My only problem with Faulkner's writing was how to pronounce *Yoknapatawpha*, the Chickasaw word that could be interpreted as "slow water," or "the people of the gentle water." *Yokkety-paw-paw? Yokata-paw-ful?* This word was Faulkner's curse on his readers. It was like talking with a mouthful of marbles.

I could not have imagined that ten years later I'd meet Malcolm Cowley at the inaugural Faulkner Conference at the University of Mississippi. Or that I would operate an indie press which its first owner named Yoknapatawpha Press. Or that together, Dean and I would publish books by William Faulkner, Willie Morris, James

Autry, Elise Winter, and Edwin Yoder Jr., publish *The Faulkner Newsletter & Yoknapatawpha Review*, establish the "Faux Faulkner" parody contest, and stage judging parties at Elaine's. And I damn well learned to pronounce *Yoknapatawpha*.

- 3 -

Cho Cho and Vicki

It was inevitable that I'd begin meeting members of Dean's family, including some who were not her blood kin. When William Faulkner married Estelle Oldham, she had two children from her previous marriage, a son, Malcolm, who was frail and would be raised by Estelle's parents, the Oldhams, and a daughter, Victoria, who had spent her childhood in Shanghai. Her nurse had nicknamed her "Cho Cho," Mandarin for "butterfly." She was an irreplaceable member of William and Estelle's family unit, a beautiful, precocious, flamboyant child to whom William dedicated his 1927 children's book, *The Wishing Tree*. He inscribed it, "For his dear friend Victoria on her eighth birthday Bill he made this Book."

Despite the affection William and Estelle lavished on Cho Cho she was by all accounts a troubled teen. Estelle packed her off to boarding school where female students learned public speaking and calligraphy. Some girls played the piano, practiced needlepoint, and made straight A's. Cho Cho ran wild. At seventeen she became pregnant. William tracked down the likely father and arranged a hasty marriage. Cho Cho named her baby Victoria (Vicki), but rumors spread that the groom was not Vicki's father. Such marriages are not meant to last. After Cho Cho's divorce, she met and married her second husband, Bill Fielden, an executive with Reynolds Tobacco who had the patience of Job and the ability to support Cho Cho. Now widowed at fifty-two, Cho Cho had inherited Bill Fielden's handsome estate. While the local impression was that Cho Cho and Dean were first cousins they were actually step-cousins separated by sixteen years.

In 1971, a year before Dean and I were married, the phone rang. It was Vicki calling from JFK Airport to let Dean know that she and her mother would be landing at Memphis Airport in a few hours. Vicki's husband, a Venezuelan named Jim Black, had died, and they were bringing him to Oxford for burial. Dean hadn't heard from Cho Cho or Vicki in years. Now they needed a ride from the airport.

Dean tried to dissuade me from accompanying her to Memphis, an hour or so northwest of Oxford. At first I assumed she didn't want to impose on me.

"This is my bucket of worms," said Dean. "I'm trying to spare you."

"Nobody has relatives as interesting as yours," I replied, tongue in cheek.

"Okay," she shrugged. "But don't say I didn't warn you." Then she added cryptically, "With an Oldham, anything goes," referring to Estelle and her kin.

This was a good time to ask the question that had been on my mind since the phone call. Why was Vicki's husband, who was of British descent, to be buried in *Mississippi*?

"Wouldn't Jim's family prefer that he be buried close to them?" I asked.

"Vicki wants to be buried next to Pappy," Dean said, "and so she wants her husband buried there, too."

In the airport lobby we waited for the step-cousins to arrive. Dean recognized Cho Cho immediately by the wobbling, pigeon-toed gait that caused her heavy breasts to sway.

"There she is," Dean whispered.

From a hundred feet I felt Cho Cho's penetrating dark eyes and wolf-like gaze. Her dark hair was worn in a bun and her lipstick was bright red. The two women embraced, then Cho Cho held Dean at arm's length while glancing curiously in my direction.

Vicki could have stepped out of Vogue. Her traveling outfit was a black blazer and green plaid skirt, sandy-blonde hair short and chic. She introduced Gillian, her two-year-old daughter. Then it was my turn. Cho Cho and Vicki shook my hand with a formality that was both cordial and intense. They were traveling with a Venezuelan executive, a friend and colleague of Vicki's husband, tall and professionally correct. At the baggage carousel he and I retrieved seven or eight suitcases. The travelers seemed to have brought enough clothes for the fall season, thus confirming Dean's suspicion that they were moving to Oxford.

"Will there be room in the car?" Dean asked when she saw the mountain of suitcases.

"Don't worry, we're renting a car," Vicki said. This spoke volumes about how Vicki and Cho Cho operated. Even with a rental car and a company executive at their disposal they expected Dean to meet them in Memphis. This would be the first of many command appearances.

Vicki asked Dean to ride in the rental with the executive while she, Cho Cho, and Gillian planned to ride in the station wagon with me. This seemed unusual. Dean was the step-cousin they hadn't seen in years. Wouldn't they want to catch up on family news? As the executive and I loaded the luggage I overheard Cho Cho whisper to Dean, "Why didn't you introduce Larry as your fiancé?" Was this remark meant for me to overhear?

"Because we're not engaged," Dean said.

"Louise thinks you are," Cho Cho replied, which told me they'd spoken with Dean's mother. Like the Mississippi River in flood, family tensions were rising.

Not only had I not proposed, but neither Dean nor I were inclined to give up our newfound independence.

I got behind the wheel of the station wagon. Cho Cho slid over next to me with little Gillian sitting next to the passenger door. Vicki sat in the backseat by herself. Though this arrangement seemed unusual I didn't give it much thought. I had driven only a short distance when Cho Cho told me to stop at a liquor store. It was neither a suggestion nor a request. She wanted a highball, and, as every southerner who grew up in the 1950s knows, that meant bourbon and Coca-Cola. Vicki seconded the drink order. I stopped and bought bourbon, Coke, ice, and cups, let down the tailgate of the station wagon and in the parking lot mixed two drinks. Watching from the rental car that had pulled in behind us Dean shrugged "I told you so."

Underway once again, the station wagon filled with cigarette smoke. Like a tag team mother and daughter grilled me. *Where was I from? Why I had moved to Oxford? Where had Dean and I met? How long had we been seeing each other?* I understood now why they wanted Dean in the other car. As the two-vehicle convoy crossed the boundary between America and berserk—*aka* the Mississippi state line—I felt Cho Cho's hand on the inside of my thigh. Fingers lingered, then were gone. I was shocked but didn't let on. What was Cho Cho up to? Was this a weird way of welcoming me to the family, or perhaps "thanking me" for driving them to Oxford? If so, she'd patted a bit too close for comfort. I drove at a steady 70 mph, steered in the center of the lane, and gave Cho Cho the benefit of the doubt. What had Dean said? *With an Oldham anything goes.*

As I soon discovered, everything Cho Cho did had to be taken with a grain of salt. What was recklessness or deviousness in others was coquettishness in her. One never knew if her flirtations were serious or merely a compulsion. The unsettling thing was that she didn't give a damn what I or anyone else thought. I began to wonder if Faulkner had based Candace "Caddy" Compson of *The Sound and the Fury* on Cho Cho, at least partially. Scholars theorize Faulkner's first cousin Sally Murry Wilkins was the prototype for Caddy, but it could have been his coquettish step-daughter who climbed a tree in muddy drawers.

William Faulkner died in 1962. By 1970 negotiations were underway for Jill Faulkner Summers to sell Rowan Oak to the University of Mississippi. Meanwhile, family members were allowed to use the home for short visits. Dr. James Webb, chair of the Ole Miss English department and volunteer curator of Rowan Oak, had left the driveway gate unlocked for us. Still in place was the "private" sign that Faulkner installed. With the rental car close behind, I parked under the porte cochere originally designed for horses and carriages. I was interested in seeing how Estelle's daughter and granddaughter would react to being back at the old homestead. Would the white columns, gallery, and railings hold powerful memories for them?

"Careful with my bags," Cho Cho called. "The one on the left is Gucci."

Dean unlocked the house. The air was stale and warm, and she asked me to open the windows. The day after Mr. Bill's funeral Estelle had famously installed a single window unit air conditioner in her upstairs bedroom. A true nineteenth-century man, William Faulkner had rejected this modern appliance. Cho Cho was to sleep in her mother's air-conditioned room. The rest of the family would make do with rotating fans. The executive and I carried luggage upstairs. The women's casual conversation filled the house with an ease of belonging. I sensed Dean's delight.

Louise soon arrived with Dean's children. After greeting Vicki and Cho Cho, the kids took Gillian by the hand and raced upstairs to explore the bedrooms. Their footfalls and laughter seemed to race across the decades, restoring Rowan Oak to what it had once been—a family home.

As a courtesy the university had provided linens and towels but no food. Cho Cho phoned the Beacon Café and ordered fried chicken livers, which I volunteered to pick up. Dean walked me to the car.

"Did you ever drive with your knees pressed together?" I asked and told her what Cho Cho did on the way from Memphis. Dean was not shocked. Nor was she angry. If Cho Cho was a nympho she was *their* nympho, and as I would soon learn, the family's way of dealing with a crisis was to pretend nothing happened. William once told Dean that her primary trait was loyalty to the family. She took this to heart.

"Now you know about my bucket of worms," she said. "Cho Cho is kind and gentle until she is crossed. Remember that."

When I returned with the fried chicken liver dinners, Cho Cho asked me to build a fire. "Pappy always kept a fire going," she said. The temperature was in the eighties. I was not offended by Cho Cho's bossy behavior but curious about her grand-dame persona. Where did she get her illusion of grandeur? Dean never displayed such hauteur, thank goodness, although on occasion showed flashes of elegant imperiousness which I suspected came from William Faulkner.

I scavenged the grounds for firewood while Cho Cho and Vicki, highballs in hand, watched from the gallery. I carried an armload of sticks and branches into the library. What to use for tinder? In an upstairs bathroom I found a magazine. Later I was scolded by the curator for destroying a "literary artifact." I assured him it was Estelle's *Harper's Bizarre* and not Faulkner's *Field and Stream* that I used to start the fire.

Cho Cho rattled ice in her glass, and I dutifully went to get a refill. When I returned, Dean was reciting one of her uncle's favorite limericks. Vicki joined in.

There once was a young man from Sparta.
A really magnificent farter.
Just by eating a bean
He'd fart God Save the Queen,
And Beethoven's Moonlight Sonata.

The children howled in amusement as if to say, "Look what adults do for fun!" Dean and Vicki hurled rhymes back and forth, evoking days gone by.

He could vary, with proper persuasion,
His fart to suit any occasion.
He could fart like a flute,
Like a lark, like a lute,
This very mellifluous Caucasian.

It was Jim Black's wake, and limericks were Dean's way of helping Vicki cope. At the same time they were subconsciously competing for Pappy's approval, exulting in his imagined chuckles as if the limericks started with him and were trickling down. This impromptu recitation was less about limericks than celebrating the Rowan Oak they'd known. Cho Cho was not the foolish middle-aged woman who'd made a pass at me but William Faulkner's beloved stepdaughter; Louise was his favorite brother's widow; Dean was the niece and ward who could do no wrong; and Vicki the quirky, unpredictable step-granddaughter. With joyful limericks Pappy's girls conjured his spirit out of firelight.

Blazing cedar branches crackled in the fireplace.

Something told me this was the only time I would experience the Rowan Oak they had known. Here were three powerful personalities—four, if one counted Dean's mother—shaped and scarred by Faulkner's fire.

As twilight filled the grounds, the women sat on the steps reminiscing about their common denominator, Pappy, whose abiding presence none of them could escape even if they wanted to. As she watched me give piggyback rides to the children, Dean remarked, "Pappy said a man's character can be judged by whether he's good with horses and children."

"Is Larry good in bed?" asked Cho Cho.

One morning after we were married Dean left me a note on the kitchen table. This was a standard method of communication since I often went to bed before she did. "Vicki and I learned our responses to men—insecure self-doubt—at/from our mothers' knees," Dean wrote. "Mine, lacking in self-confidence, fearful of rejection, but totally trusting in male friendship prized far above that of other women. Cho Cho and Vicki however seemed to dabble in men."

This complex and haunted homecoming was my induction into the Faulkner family. For a few hours I experienced the Rowan Oak that Dean had known, warm, enchanting, and eccentric. As she

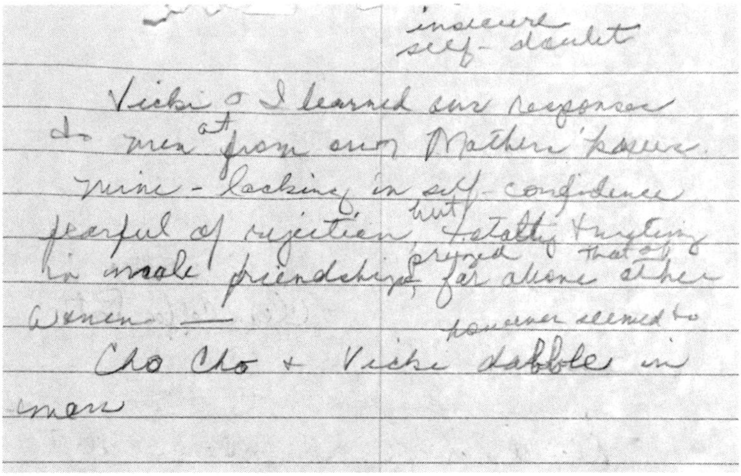
insecure
self-doubt
Vicki & I learned our responses to men at from our Mother's house.
mine - lacking in self-confidence fearful of rejection, but totally trusting in male friendships, prized that of far above other women —
however seemed to
Cho Cho + Vicki dabble in men

and I walked to the car she stopped me, and standing under the cedars said, "I wish I could have given you to Pappy. He'd have made you his right-hand man. You would have been the best of friends."

Two days later we buried Jim Black less than fifty feet from William Faulkner. Within a week Cho Cho had purchased a house on St. Andrew's Circle, furnished it, and issued an invitation for drinks. Dean's mother welcomed the distraction. Now Louise had allies and someplace to go. Dean worried that the three of them were plotting against us.

"Don't borrow trouble," I said.

It took Vicki a month to make her move. She got all gussied up, in Dean's words, and came to my apartment behind Oxford's Church of Christ. When her Chrysler pulled into my driveway it set off alarms. I phoned Dean while watching through the blinds. "What is Vicki up to?"

"Keep her at arm's length," Dean warned.

Leaving the phone off the hook so that Dean could hear, I greeted Vicki through the screened door.

"Hi, Vicki," I said. "What can I do for you?"

"I brought you a book," she said, waiting for me to invite her in.

"Thanks," I said. "But would you mind leaving it on the steps? I'm in the middle of a project." I shut the door, and even before I picked up the phone I could hear Dean laughing.

"If you had let her in," she said, "I'd soon be hearing about your delightful afternoon together."

I flicked the venetian blinds and saw Vicki toss the book into the bushes. After she drove off I retrieved the book. It was Camus's *The Stranger*. Among other things, Vicki was working on a master's in French.

The step-cousins were not done yet. A week later Cho Cho and Vicki held a joint housewarming party. Maids in starched uniforms served Bloody Marys and quiche. Cho Cho drew me into the parlor and squeezed into a love seat next to me.

"Larry, where can I get a man?" she asked.

I almost said, "Check your guest list."

With an unremitting stare, she looked me in the eye and said, "My body is still good and I can screw like hell." I stared at my shoes and wondered what William Faulkner would have said. His fictional Caddy smelled of trees and was last seen in a Nazi general's touring car whereas the real one was sitting next to me on a love seat reeking of vodka and cigarettes.

"I hear single men attend plays," I offered. "Or bridge tournaments, or square dances . . ."

"Square dances!" Cho Cho stiffened. "Do you find me *ordinary*?"

"Of course not," I said and meant it. Cho Cho was anything but ordinary, though just then the image of her at a square dance, pigeon-toed in full skirt and bobbysocks while costumed dancers whirled about her, appealed to me. "In New York, one calls an escort service!" She was now furious. I felt a twinge of sympathy for a couple of seconds until she added, "Are there houseboys in Oxford?"

"Memphis will have better odds," I said and got the hell out of the parlor.

A few years later Cho Cho was diagnosed with cancer and given a month to live. The news took everyone by surprise. I think we forgot she was mortal. Dean rushed to Cho Cho's house and vowed to stay at her side.

"Pappy said being alive is just getting ready to be dead for a very long time," Cho Cho said.

Every day for two weeks Dean read to her, prepared meals, and tried in myriad small ways to offer comfort. For once, Vicki was not jealous but went about emptying ashtrays and collecting empty glasses. When it counted they were like sisters.

Vicki talked her mother into allowing a priest to perform last rites. He prayed while Cho Cho chain-smoked. After he left none of us could think of anything to say. Gillian, who by that time was in the first grade, climbed in bed with her grandmother. A child's love is the best medicine. Cho Cho began to reminisce.

"Do you remember how I used to brush the knots out of your hair and pull the braids tight?" she asked. They did, both Vicki and Dean.

"I hid under the staircase!" Dean recalled.

Cho Cho laughed until she had a coughing spasm. "What about the Halloween when I played a ghost waving a sheet over my head?" she said. "Or that night when you both were asleep, and I pretended to be 'Judith' playing Chopin's *Minute Waltz* on the piano. You two were scared to death."

Cho Cho coughed up blood. Dean fetched a towel. Vicki poured a glass of vodka. Her mother drank it, lay back with a sigh, and closed her eyes.

Victoria Oldham Fielden left instructions to have her ashes scattered in the Mississippi River, some seventy-five miles from Oxford. Vicki compromised by dropping them into Hickahala Creek, which flowed into the Tallahatchie, which flowed into the Yazoo, which emptied into the Mississippi. It was just a slightly longer journey.

As the ashes disappeared into the swirling water Cho Cho's friend Louis Dollarhide, the same professor who taught the *Beowulf* seminar where Dean and I met, read from Cho Cho's favorite poem, "Invictus":

Out of the night that covers me,
Black as the Pit from pole to pole,
I thank whatever gods may be
For my unconquerable soul.

Simplified Family Tree

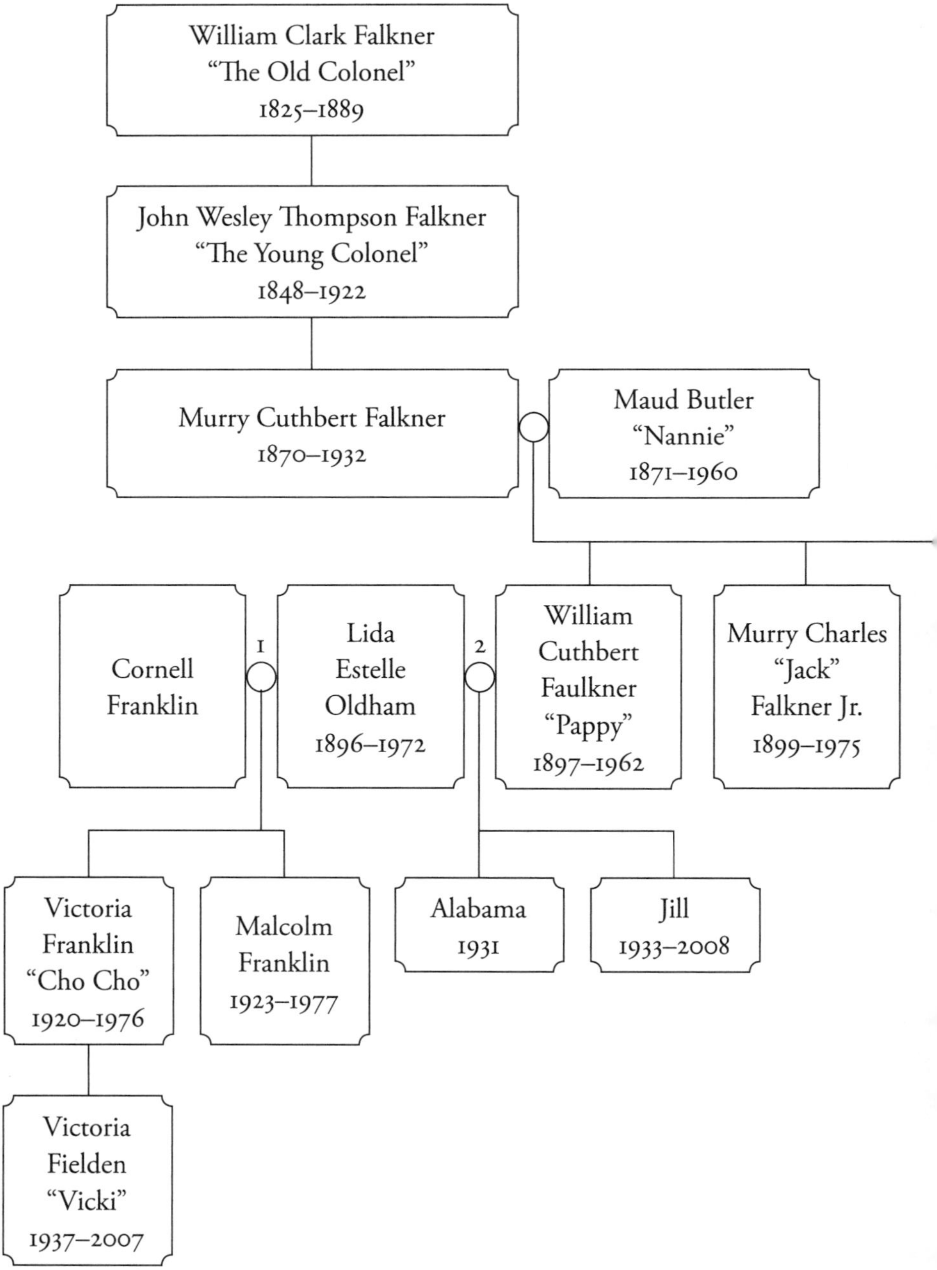

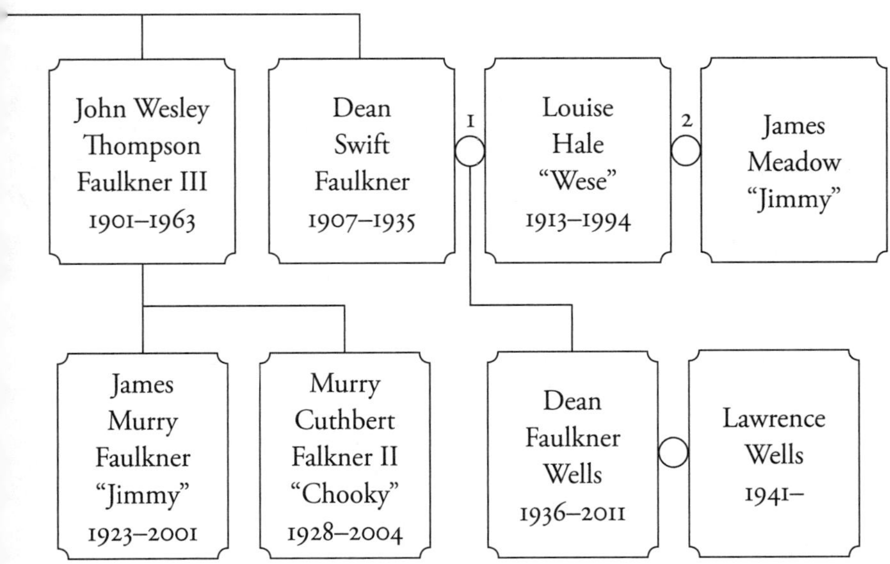

John Wesley Thompson Faulkner III 1901–1963
Dean Swift Faulkner 1907–1935
1
Louise Hale "Wese" 1913–1994
2
James Meadow "Jimmy"
James Murry Faulkner "Jimmy" 1923–2001
Murry Cuthbert Falkner II "Chooky" 1928–2004
Dean Faulkner Wells 1936–2011
Lawrence Wells 1941–

\- 4 -

Elephant in the Room

To those born without it genius can be a forbidding heritage. When William Faulkner received the Nobel Prize his kith and kin became trapped in his shadow. After his death Dean observed that she and her relatives built walls shielding themselves not just from outsiders but from one another. The cousins and step-cousins included Dean, Faulkner's daughter, Jill, his stepchildren, Victoria and Malcolm, and his nephews Jimmy and Chooky. They were not a close-knit family but prone to estrangements and slow to forgive.

As an air force wife for thirteen years, Dean was spared the reflected glare of her uncle's fame. The air force community didn't care if she was Faulkner's niece. Her husband's rank was all that mattered. This anonymity suited Dean, who was self-effacing yet sophisticated, opposite qualities that came naturally to her.

William and Estelle's daughter, Jill, shunned publicity and rarely made statements about her father. As a young child, she adjusted to her parents' addiction to alcohol. On rare occasions when William and Estelle weren't physically able to carry out their responsibilities, Jill directed the household staff, planned menus, and made sure her parents were dressed and at table when meals were served. These experiences forced her to grow up before her time. For the rest of her life, dignity and order would be her first priorities.

Jill inherited her father's immense reserve along with his dry wit. Though reluctant to speak about him she gave a candid interview

in the award-winning 1978 Mississippi ETV documentary, *A Life on Paper*. She recalled an occasion when her father took to his bed during a binge. She entered his bedroom at Rowan Oak and attempted to remove his whiskey bottle. William clasped the bottle to his chest muttering, "No one remembers Shakespeare's child."

For decades Jill kept this painful memory to herself. When this admission was broadcast on national television, Dean and I were horrified that Jill had endured such a cruel slight. Dean praised her cousin's courage and candor observing, "She couldn't hold it in any longer. It had to come out."

William loved Jill unconditionally yet assumed that she would always live up to his expectations. Dean, however, was not under the same pressure. She was the miracle child, the living embodiment of her dead father. "I was the second coming!" she wrote in her memoir. And for William and Maud she could do no wrong. Jill and Vicki couldn't compete with William's grief for his lost brother. As children they resented the special treatment Dean received, and this sibling rivalry stalked them into adulthood.

Vicki ran hot and cold toward Dean, who tolerated her out of family loyalty. Vicki's parents parked her at Rowan Oak when it suited them, and Louise regularly sent Dean there to escape her alcoholic and abusive stepfather. Like Vicki, Dean needed approval and consistency. That each found it at Rowan Oak is testimony to William's devotion. When Dean was eight, he adopted her and became her legal guardian.

William felt a heavy responsibility. He'd given his brother Dean the biplane in which he died. William made a vow that he would rear his niece Dean in his brother's place, and she grew up calling him Pappy. For Dean three places—Maud's home in Oxford, the farm of her Hale grandparents, and Rowan Oak—were havens of order and stability.

To understand the girls of Rowan Oak one has to consider how they were shaped by a fierce, unending competition for William's approval. Jill retreated behind reserve. Vicki slipped into paranoia. Dean was by nature loyal to her cousin and step-cousin. If the girls had bonded for life they would have been prepared for what awaited them, but this was not meant to be.

Vicki arrived at Rowan Oak with a note pinned to her dress that read, "Take me to William Faulkner, Oxford Miss." At the time, Cho Cho and her husband, Bill, were relocating to the Philippines, where he was regional sales manager for Reynolds Tobacco.

Vicki was Estelle's granddaughter and Jill's niece. Periodically William and Estelle housed and cared for Vicki just as they had taken care of Cho Cho and Malcolm.

To Jill and Dean, Vicki seemed quirky and very sure of herself. She had a British accent, spoke French, and was determined to win at cards or croquet. One thinks of Truman Capote's character "Dill," in *To Kill a Mockingbird* ("I may be little but I'm old!"), who hides a sensitive nature behind a prim facade. Vicki also had a Boo Radley side.

Dean's childhood friend, Sandra Baker Moore, who grew up next door to Rowan Oak, remembers that Vicki loved Gothic stories.

"Vicki introduced us to the horror stories of slaves tortured by a white woman in New Orleans in the 1800s," Sandra told me in an interview. "She would chase us around the house, reading it aloud to us over our protests, wouldn't stop until we threatened to go home. No sooner would we sit down than she might start reciting Poe's *The Raven*. She was so proud of her black six-toed cat. Told us he was the devil himself. That cat would lie in wait for us on the stairs and hiss and scratch at our ankles as we went up to Vicki's room. Dean was terrified of that cat."

Every spring William put up a croquet court and left it in place until first frost. He enjoyed playing cutthroat croquet with his girls. Mortal combat under the cedars. No quarter given. One day during a croquet match a thunderstorm blew up. The cedar trees bent under heavy gusts. A jagged tower of lightning stood on the horizon. Rain pelting their faces Jill, Dean, and Vicki waited for permission to go inside, but until William released them, even the closest lightning strike couldn't make them run for cover. Drenched to the skin, hair plastered by rain, ready to die for his approval, they waited. Faulkner gripped his croquet mallet and continued playing. Something, who knows what?—being a role model to whom courage was the most important human quality?—made him wait to see who would be the first to break and run. Only when the skies opened up did he give in. As lightning seared the sky, Pappy's girls, soaking wet, severely pleased, followed him to shelter. It never occurred to them to question why he had risked their safety. After all, they were cut from the same cloth. After Dean's account of this incident, I finally understood why Pappy's girls gave no quarter.

One Friday evening Dean and I stopped by Vicki's for a drink. We were informally engaged. Our contentment must have irritated Vicki because when Dean mentioned that she had a mild headache Vicki produced a sample case containing hundreds of pills she'd brought from Venezuela where her husband, Jim, had been a pharmaceutical manufacturer. She offered Dean what she claimed to be a mild painkiller. Knowing Vicki's malfeasance I was concerned. Dean dismissed my suspicions, took the pills, and ten minutes after we left she passed out in the car.

I was furious at Vicki. Dean could have died. I kept nudging her to keep her awake. She refused to go to the emergency room. Frantic that she might slip into a coma—and having no clue what tranquillizer or heavy painkiller Vicki had given her—I walked Dean around the block until she came to her senses. We sat up past midnight until the medication, whatever it was, wore off.

A year later Vicki drove a permanent wedge between Jill and Dean. The occasion was Jill's sale of Rowan Oak to the University of Mississippi. Vicki hosted a reception at her home and invited university faculty and officials to what was, in effect, a Faulkner family celebration, yet left Dean and me off the invitation list. When Jill asked why Dean wasn't present, Vicki feigned ignorance. We learned of this from Louise, who casually mentioned it a few days later. Dean was horrified. *Why hadn't her mother explained her absence to Jill?* And for that matter, Dean wondered, how could Louise have remained at the party knowing Vicki had snubbed her daughter? Either this hadn't occurred to Louise or, more likely, having her own ax to grind she had been content to remain silent. When Dean most needed loyalty, her mother let her down.

Within a week Dean phoned Jill in Charlottesville to explain. Yet Jill seized upon the faux-snub as an excuse to break off relations. Jill and Vicki had apparently forgotten what William told the girls whenever he caught them fighting: "*You're better than that.*"

Until Jill's death in 2008 she and Dean spoke to each other twice. The first occasion was in 1981 when Dean visited Charlottesville, Virginia, to promote her book, *The Great American Writers' Cookbook*. Not wanting to "bother" Jill, she wasn't planning to phone.

"You can't be in Charlottesville and not contact Jill," I said, badgering her until she phoned and invited Jill to lunch.

"I ride on Tuesdays," Jill curtly replied. Not even a no thanks, or sorry I can't go. For a few seconds they stayed on the line waiting for the other to speak. Then Jill, who was master of foxhounds at Farmington Hill Hunt, hung up. Dean was furious at me for putting her in that position.

"At least you tried," I said.

Their last encounter came at a donors luncheon at Rowan Oak. They hadn't seen each other in three decades. After the meal Dean approached Jill and stuck out her hand.

"I'm Dean," she said. It was a simple and elegant way to break the ice if Jill was wise enough to accept it.

"I know who you are!" was all that Jill said.

Pappy's girls parted on the grounds of Rowan Oak never to see each other again.

- 5 -

Sibling Rivals

WILLIAM'S ONLY NEPHEWS WERE THE SONS OF HIS BROTHER, John Faulkner. Jimmy and Murry C. ("Chooky") were separated by two years and the spelling of their name. Chooky spelled it "Falkner" as had his grandfather and great-grandfather, while Jimmy, following his father John's example, added a *u*.

John Faulkner changed the spelling before his first novel, *Men Working*, was published in 1941. His novel *Dollar Cotton*, 1942, was followed by a series of rustic comedies beginning with *Cabin Road* (1951) in the manner of Erskine Caldwell's *Tobacco Road*. Published posthumously *My Brother, Bill* (1963) was a memoir of growing up as the brother of a Nobel laureate.

Over the years a legacy of violence haunted the Faulkner males. It began with the "Old Colonel," William Clark Falkner, of Ripley, Mississippi, William Faulkner's great-grandfather and namesake. The colonel fought in two duels and was killed by a political rival in the streets of Ripley. His grandson, Murry Falkner (William's father), was shot in a fight, the bullet lodging in his throat and cutting off his windpipe. Called to the scene his mother, Sallie Murry Falkner made Murry swallow asphidity, a concoction of strong herbs, which caused him to throw up and dislodged the bullet. On another occasion Murry attacked a man in front of his hardware store and would have beaten him to death if bystanders hadn't stepped in.

Jimmy Faulkner physically resembled his uncle William, but the similarity ended there. He flew Corsairs in WWII in the Pacific theater of war and had a hair-trigger temper. When I met him in 1971 he was a reserve fighter pilot in search of a target. Once, when I removed a badly weathered "FALKNER" concrete gate stone from our front yard to save the lettering (including the famous "backwards N") from erosion, Jimmy threatened to sic the sheriff on me. He owned a portion of Miss Maud's property and had every right to object. But in my experience, Jimmy consistently took offense at the least excuse.

It appeared that he had anger-management problems. The inherited belief that Faulkners were always right produced in the brothers a bulletproof arrogance. There was no arguing with Jimmy and Chooky. Once they took a position they never wavered.

In 1978 the heralded PBS series, *The American Short Story*, adapted Faulkner's story, "Barn Burning," for television. The story introduces Abner Snopes as a character and represents Faulkner's archetypal collision of haves and have-nots. Jimmy Faulkner was cast in the role of "Major de Spain," a well-to-do landowner. Tommy Lee Jones in his first starring role played the barn-burner, Abner Snopes.

Producer Calvin Skaggs told us he was pleased to have a nephew of William Faulkner in the film. Jimmy was well suited for the part, said Skaggs, because he was "more 18th Century than 19th." Major de Spain's role in the film is to react with outrage to Snopes's provocation. Perhaps Skaggs sensed the violent streak behind Jimmy's polite southern manner.

Tommy Lee Jones was in character when he arrived at Memphis Airport, reportedly spitting tobacco and grinding it into the carpet of the car sent to fetch him. Dean and I were present on location when a crucial scene was filmed. In the scene Abner Snopes ground horse excrement into de Spain's rug with his heel while Major de Spain stood at the top of a staircase watching Snopes ruin the rug. Jimmy had a single line, something like "What do you think you're doing!" and then he was to rush downstairs to confront Snopes.

It was a simple scene, but each time the camera rolled Jimmy lost his temper at the sight of Tommy Lee's insolent smile. Jones, a former Harvard football player from West Texas, was possibly descended from Texas rangers or desperados or both. Hence his role came naturally to him as well. His expression as he stared up at Jimmy epitomized a rising middle class, while Jimmy personified the slave-owning Old South.

Here were Faulkner's extremes of Yoknapatawpha County, landed gentry and sharecropper on a collision course. Jimmy must have done ten takes. Finally, too tired to care, he delivered the line in the soft, lethal manner that director Peter Werner wanted.

Chooky Falkner didn't share the "u" in his brother's surname or violent temper but he was locally famous for standing his ground. In civilian life his occupation was insurance agent, but his true calling was the Mississippi National Guard. During the 1962 Ole Miss riot over the admission of James Meredith, the first African American student to break the color barrier at the University of Mississippi, Chooky distinguished himself as commander of the Oxford National Guard unit. Like most white conservatives he had mixed feelings about James Meredith's right to enroll at the University of Mississippi, but when President Kennedy federalized the Mississippi National Guard, Chooky took the oath of allegiance and swore to defend the Constitution of the United States.

As the National Guard convoy arrived on campus a mob of demonstrators attacked Chooky's jeep. A concrete block smashed his right elbow. Ignoring the pain, he stationed his guardsmen between the mob and the US marshals. Minutes later he heard the rattle of an approaching bulldozer.

Alone in the street, his broken arm in a sling fashioned from an ammunition belt, Captain Falkner faced the oncoming 'dozer, behind which crouched a dozen armed rioters like infantry behind a tank. At first the driver slowed down, then raising the bulldozer's blade he accelerated. At the last second he braked with the blade hovering a foot from Captain Falkner's face. In that split second Chooky recognized the bulldozer driver.

I believe that each brother in his own way was trying to emerge from his uncle William's shadow and distinguish himself for good or ill. Chooky received recognition for his courageous actions. He was commended by the National Guard and at the end of his career was promoted to brigadier general. Nobody talks about Jimmy's part in the riot.

The 1962 integration crisis at Ole Miss has been called the "last battle of the Civil War" when brother fought against brother. Divisions within the Faulkner family had first surfaced with Maud's death in 1960. The cousins' grandmother left behind a loosely worded, handwritten will bequeathing specific items to three of her four grandchildren. Having overlooked Chooky, she added a postscript stating that he could have "anything he wanted." Chooky took the offer literally. He parked a pickup in the front yard and began hauling away furniture and paintings. Louise, who had stayed with Maud as a companion, was still a resident in the house. She reported this activity to Dean, who was living in South Carolina. Chooky subsequently was persuaded to sign a quitclaim.

Jimmy, to whom primogeniture was the ultimate law of human existence, claimed the family Bible and any other memorabilia that he felt belonged to the eldest male. Jill, who inherited Rowan Oak and its furnishings, could not be bothered with the division of Maud's property. It was beneath her dignity.

In 1974, Vicki and Dean participated in a family panel at the inaugural Faulkner Conference at the University of Mississippi. Bishop Hall Auditorium was filled to capacity. I sat in the aisle wondering how Pappy's girls would perform together. It had only been a year since Vicki gave the reception and caused the schism between Jill and Dean. What I didn't know was that the sibling rivalry between Pappy's girls was about to come to a head. Vicki was a trained actress. Dean was shy and self-effacing, or so I thought.

Before Vicki could react to a question from the audience Dean began to reminisce about what it was like to grow up at Rowan Oak. Vicki interrupted several times, saying, "That's not how I remember it!"

I sat electrified in the aisle. Dean had been hiding her voice of authority. Was this the same mother who made school lunches and ironed her daughters' clothes at six a.m.? The high school French teacher whose students sang Christmas carols *en francais*? Or the niece and ward of a Nobel laureate who'd given her a reading list expecting her to read every book, who laid out her course of study and handpicked her professors? This was the moment Dean acknowledged her birthright and in effect accepted life under Pappy's shadow.

When the program ended, the audience swarmed three-deep around her. One could hardly blame Vicki for being jealous. She was an Oldham. Dean was a Faulkner. I remember thinking, "Dean will never be the same again." Even Willie Morris, who would later lecture in the same Bishop Hall Auditorium, didn't receive the bone-deep affection the audience showered on Dean that day.

She was the Faulkner who came out of hiding.

- 6 -

Wese

LOUISE HALE FAULKNER MEADOW WAS TWENTY-TWO WHEN her first husband, Dean Swift Faulkner, was killed. Her subsequent eighteen-year marriage to Jimmy Meadow, a talented but neurotic journalist, nearly destroyed her. Upon her second husband's death in 1958 Louise returned to Oxford and moved in with her former mother-in-law. When Maud died in 1960 William allowed Louise to live in Maud's home. Her elderly parents and her sister, Clara Mae, moved in with her. Louise was hired as social director at the campus YMCA, where a friendly circle of graduate students soon dubbed her "MoWese."

Dean's return to Oxford in 1970 ended her mother's sojourn in Miss Maud's house and initiated a twenty-year war between mother and daughter. Louise's ill-concealed hostility toward Dean morphed into opposition to our relationship, which made it difficult to befriend my future mother-in-law. When sober and in a good humor she was cordial. When she was in her cups all bets were off.

Not long after Dean moved back to Oxford, Pete and Jane, a married couple she'd known at Hilton Head, came to visit her. Excited to be hosting her friends Dean unpacked her silver and crystal, ordered a cake and a floral centerpiece. Learning that her daughter was giving a dinner party Louise was furious that she hadn't been invited. She began drinking and phoned Dean multiple times.

"*Whass goin' on?*" she shouted into the telephone.

"It's all right," Jane assured Dean when told about the situation. "We're each allowed one crazy relative." No sooner had Dean, her children, and her guests sat down to dinner than Louise staggered into the house. She dragged a kitchen chair to the dining room table.

"Well, it looks like Dean doesn't want her friends to meet her mother!" she declared.

"Nice to meet you," said Jane. "This is our first visit to Oxford. What a lovely town!"

"You can have Oxford," Louise replied. "Have you ever been kicked out of your home?" She attempted to light a cigarette with a candle. The candlestick fell over. The children shrieked. Dean snatched it up before the tablecloth burned. Louise cackled. And as if this were a signal everyone at the table began yelling.

"*Weeser, go home!*" yelled the children.

Louise rested her head on the table and passed out. Dean's candlelight dinner lay in ruins.

The next day Dean arranged a picnic at Rowan Oak. It was a cool, sunny day in October. Dean and Jane spread a picnic blanket on the lawn. Pete uncorked the champagne. As they raised their glasses two figures struggled up the cedar-lined driveway: Louise and Dean's babysitter, Chrissy Price, the housekeeper at Rowan Oak and widow of Faulkner's groom and handyman, Andrew Price.

"Well, *la de dah*," Louise sneered. Chrissy straightaway asked if she could help serve lunch, which was her way of explaining why she'd left the children unattended. Dean saw what was going on. Louise had ordered Chrissy to accompany her to Rowan Oak. With no babysitter Dean would be forced to return home. Hanging on to Chrissy for balance, Louise smirked. Pete grabbed Louise by the shoulders.

"You're destroying your daughter's happiness!" he shouted.

Dean tried to intervene, and all three were locked in a wretched embrace. Shrieking, Louise toppled over, taking Dean down with her.

"She's winning," Jane observed.

I met Louise in 1971 shortly before Dean and I went to Memphis to pick up Vicki and Cho Cho. I'd begun helping out around the house, running errands and delivering the children to movie theater or skating rink. Returning from one such delivery and assuming Dean was alone I opened the front door and called, "*Take me, I'm yours!*"

"We're in the kitchen!" Dean answered.

We? I thought. Chastened, I entered the kitchen where Louise Hale Faulkner Meadow raised her glass in a toast.

"Take *me*!" she said.

"This is my mother," Dean said. "Louise, this is Larry."

At fifty-nine Louise was a tall, handsome woman made thin by wrath and bourbon. Her hair was electric blue with a lacquered finish. She took a drag on her cigarette and blew a smoke ring at me.

"Y'all studyin' tonight?" she asked. I thought fast. Dean obviously had told her we were study-mates.

"Yes, ma'am." I felt like a sophomore lying to my girlfriend's mother.

"Did you bring your lecture notes?" Dean said, playing along.

"I was living in this house," Louise muttered, "before she came back for graduate school, but that's water under the bridge." She lit another cigarette and dropped the still-burning match in an ashtray. "I can't believe the marriage is over. Dean was a lovely bride."

"Oh, come off it, Mama!" Dean said.

The match reignited cigarette stubs in the ashtray. The past was on fire. I extinguished the butts. Louise didn't explain, but then no one in Dean's family ever explained. Over the kitchen door hung a wooden plank on which Dean's grandmother, the original un-explainer Maud, had printed "*DON'T COMPLAIN, DON'T EXPLAIN.*"

"So, is that the family motto?" I said just making conversation.

Louise squinted through cigarette smoke. "Remember Tommy? A terrific, terrific catch." The implication was that Dean could do better than what's-his-name.

"Tommy is married or have you forgotten?" Dean said.

If Louise wanted to marry Dean off and get her out of Miss Maud's house, that opportunity had come and gone only the day before when one of Dean's former classmates dropped by. I had never met him but it was obvious that as an undergraduate he'd had a crush on her. I couldn't tell, however, if she'd reciprocated.

The descendant of a Confederate general, he was a bank president with grand ambitions. If he married a Faulkner he might even run for governor of Mississippi. He appeared, unannounced, when I happened to be at Dean's. She asked me to see who was at the door. The would-be suitor was not pleased to be greeted by a bearded guy. *Was Dean hanging out with hippies?* She introduced me as "a friend at Ole Miss."

Dean was enjoying having two rivals compete over her, not to make me jealous but to show me that she was sought-after—as if I didn't know that already. She was of that breed of gentlewoman who is refreshed by male attention. This may have been partly due to her aunt Estelle's influence. Estelle once told her, "Always try to be charming. Men appreciate that in a woman."

"Don't make a bad decision," the ex-boyfriend blurted. "This is the most important decision of your life, Dean. Don't make a big mistake."

By presuming to lecture her he had shot himself in the foot. It was all I could do to keep a straight face. After a pregnant silence Dean asked after his wife, which was the kiss of death. Desperate, he invited her to dinner. As if to prove her independence—to both of us—she let the invitation hang in the air.

"I'll stay with the kids if you go out," I offered. This was a calculated risk. A glimmer of a smile passed over her face. There was affection in the glance but also a challenge: *Don't hem me in.*

Obviously, Dean hadn't told Louise about the former boyfriend's recent visit or her mother would have been promoting this well-to-do bank president who might have swept Dean away. Louise jabbed her cigarette in the air, inadvertently creating another smoke ring.

"Remember that handsome heir to the Little Rock Coca-Cola fortune?" she babbled. "The one that went to West Point. You could have any man you wanted. Remember the dance contest? You and Eddie what's-his-name?"

"So I could dance!" Dean exhibited a practiced patience with her mother. In time I would discover why.

After Dean Swift Faulkner was killed, Louise moved in with her parents in the country. She married Jimmy Meadow in 1940 without knowing what she was getting herself into. Dean grew up with a schizophrenic, abusive stepfather. To teach her to drive Louise had to borrow a friend's car. As Dean practiced driving, Louise told her stories about her father—his strength, gentleness, and sense of humor.

At the time of Dean's plane crash they'd been married less than two years. In the red biplane that William gave Dean, the young couple flew over West Memphis or Clarksdale, Louise tossing promotional leaflets from the plane announcing an upcoming air show. Louise's primary role as a mother was to teach Dean who she was and where she came from. In the meantime, a very different Louise than the caring mother who'd raised the woman I loved was staring bullets at me.

"What happened to *your* marriage, if I may ask?" she said.

"Mama, please!"

"My ex and I split," I said, taken aback.

"Oh, my, the modern world of ex's and splits. Whatever happened to stick-to-it-ness?"

Dean's warning glance screamed *Don't take the bait!* "Mama, don't you have a bridge game?"

Louise struggled to her feet and, refusing Dean's helping hand, staggered into the dining room. Then as if she'd remembered something she stopped and turned. Dean blocked the door to keep her from returning to the kitchen. They grappled while I, a noncombatant, stood with hands behind my back. There was no way I was cutting into this mother-daughter dance. Louise cursed under her breath, and Dean stormed up the hallway leaving me alone with my future mother-in-law. The referee had left the arena. A deep silence settled over the dining room where William Faulkner had proofed his greatest novel *Absalom, Absalom!* while Louise, newly widowed at twenty-two, had slept in the bedroom across the hall.

"*This is un-real,*" she said. I couldn't have agreed more. When it became obvious Dean was not coming back, Louise hobbled to the front door. I assisted her down the steps. We cut across the yard to her Buick coupe parked at the service station next door. She slid behind the wheel but did not start the engine. In case further assistance was required I waited. Louise stared into space. The dry smell of autumn hung in the air. Venus was rising. I returned to the house.

Dean was sitting on her bed looking miserable. Louise had driven home her grievance and her "ungrateful" daughter had kicked her out of the house. Without a word Dean handed me her car keys. It was time to pick up the kids at the skating rink. As we left the house Louise started the engine and whipped the green Buick into the street with a shriek of burning rubber. Before I could back out Dean laid a hand on my arm.

"She's blocking us," Dean said. Indeed, Louise had made a U-turn and pulled athwart the driveway.

"Doesn't she have a bridge game?" I said.

"I made that up!"

Louise parked by the curb and waited. I pulled up next to her, reached across Dean to roll down the window, and asked Louise if she needed assistance. At some point we were going to have to bury the hatchet. It was not too soon to start.

She gestured impatiently at me to drive on. Halfway down the block I turned around in a parking lot and started back toward University Avenue. To my surprise Louise swerved into my lane. At first I thought she was joking. Then the poetic justice hit me. We had been on a collision course from the moment we met.

“Don’t play chicken with my mother!” Dean warned. I twisted the steering wheel and like spooked mules the two vehicles shied away from each other. I caught a glimpse of blue hair and fury.

We rode to the skating rink where I parked in the pick-up lane. Kids were pouring out of the theater. In piled Diane, Paige, and Jon filling the car with youth and exuberance. Now we were five, or six counting the lady in the Buick behind us.

- 7 -

Family Ghosts

On the day that her stepfather died, Dean was driving across Kentucky with her first husband, Jon. Entering a restaurant Dean noticed a man seated alone at a corner table who closely resembled Jimmy Meadow, whose face was engrained in her memory. The last she'd heard of Meadow he was homeless in Chicago.

Turning on her heel she left the restaurant. No sooner had she returned to her motel room than the phone rang. Louise was calling with the news that Jimmy Meadow had died that afternoon.

Human memory begins with smell. Dean's earliest memory of Louise was the smell of the outdoors. Dean was living at the farm of Louise's parents, Sanford and Pearl Hale. Late every afternoon Louise would return from work and scoop up her toddler. Dean identified her mother with the cool smell of fresh air. Likewise, her first memory of her grandmother, Nannie, was the scent of lilac talcum.

I believe that Dean was Maud's favorite grandchild. Both stood ramrod straight as if aligned with the earth's axis. Both were fatherless. Dean never knew her father and Maud was sixteen when her father, Charlie, ran away with another woman. The difference was that Maud's loss made her bitter.

On Christmas eve, 1887, Charlie Butler, Oxford's marshal and tax collector, disappeared with his mistress and $3,000 in city tax revenues, Maud and her mother, Lelia Dean Butler, spent the next half century living down the shame. Knowing how it felt to be fatherless, Maud was extra protective of Dean, which to a spiritualist might explain Maud's supernatural "visitations" at 510 South Lamar.

One afternoon the two of us were alone in Miss Maud's house. Dean turned in the central hallway, not alarmed but with pleasure saying, "Nannie's here!"

Several times over the years Dean would stop in the hallway that seemed designed to channel family ghosts. She would invite me to smell Maud's lilac talcum. One step forward and I smelled it. One step back and the odor disappeared. I had the distinct feeling not only of a ghostly presence but a mischievous one. Being allowed to smell the talcum, I wanted to believe, was tantamount to receiving Maud's blessing. Surely I couldn't have done so if the spirit—her presence, let's say—didn't want me to.

In the same place in the hallway, we experienced other talcum encounters. Each time Dean reacted with a joyful alertness, as if she and Nannie were resuming a conversation: *By the way, Lamb, as I was saying—*

Having dealt with her father's death at a very early age gave Dean a heightened spirituality. She was happy when a visitation, or what passed for one, occurred. She seemed to have a foot in the worlds of the living and the dead.

Although I can't say beyond a doubt that Miss Maud's spirit appeared to us as the smell of lilac talcum, I can attest that to stand next to Dean at such a moment was to believe.

Not long after Maud's ghost came calling, Dean and I received a visit from the most important person in her life. "Pappy's" visitation seemed not only real but, given the circumstances, inevitable. It happened the night we sat on Dean's front steps trying to come to terms with our future. Faulkner's presence in our bedrooms half a mile apart, in different forms, gave us the sense that we weren't alone in making that decision.

Lovers develop a sixth sense about each other. I often could anticipate what Dean was thinking. For example, if she were about to say, "Let's go to the movies!" I might pipe up, "I've been wanting to see *The French Connection*." If she were on the verge of proposing a dinner party I might say, "It's been a while since we had so-and-so over." Either we were born on the same wave length, or our planets were aligned, or we spent too much time together.

In the summer of 1972 we arrived at the fail-safe point when lovers must decide whether to get married or go their separate ways. Late one night we sat on Dean's front steps taking stock. The good news was that we were together. What we did tomorrow or a year from now didn't matter. If we were lucky enough to have fallen in love, marriage seemed an unnecessary complication. The bad news was that in the seventies courtship was one thing, living in sin was another. Tongues wagged. Mothers wouldn't let daughters invite Diane and Paige to birthday parties lest the Scarlet Woman appear with them.

Society put a time limit on sexual relationships. Everyone knew we were a couple—or "cohabiting," as one of our professors put it at a cocktail party. That Dean's daughters were being snubbed was impacting their emotional development. Something had to give.

With no answers in sight I kissed Dean goodnight and walked to my apartment across town. A couple of hours later I woke up. Someone was watching me. Filling the window frame was William Faulkner's face as well defined as a photograph. After I got over my surprise I realized that the image was formed by leaf-shadow cast by a streetlight on the window shade. Yet there was no mistaking the white, starched mustache, the eyes dark and profound. All that was missing was a pipe. For the better part of an hour Faulkner and I gazed at each other, *mano a mano*, his black eyes burning into my soul. Was this ghostly presence a warning or a benediction? Finally I fell asleep.

The next morning Dean and I met at the student union. We'd barely set our coffee cups on the table when I burst out, "I think I saw Pappy last night!"

"Was it at three o'clock?" she said calmly.

At the same time that I saw Faulkner at my window she was awakened by the smell of pipe smoke, a Dunhill blend so distinctive she recognized it in her sleep. She and Vicki used to steal his pipe tobacco and roll their own. She followed the smell of smoke down the hallway into the dining room half-expecting to see Pappy puffing his pipe at the table where he proofed *Absalom, Absalom!*

When she turned on the light the air was clear, though she could still smell the familiar pipe smoke. When Dean's father died on November 10, 1935, William brought Louise, who was five months pregnant, to live with Maud until the baby was born. For a week William slept on a cot in the dining room and helped his mother care for his sister-in-law. At the same time he was under a publisher's deadline to finish proofing *Absalom* galleys. No doubt it came as a relief to have something to do other than grieve. For Dean the ambient pipe smoke, perhaps embedded in the wallpaper was directly connected with her father's death. She returned to bed wondering why her uncle's spirit had chosen that particular night to manifest itself.

Now she knew.

On Wednesday night Dean parked in my driveway behind my Kharmann Ghia convertible. When I opened the door to let her in, the smell of frying bacon made her smile. My bachelor's apartment at Mrs. Lucille Bailey's home behind the Church of Christ had an unusual layout. Mrs. Bailey had walled in her patio and connected the garage apartment to the house. The living room featured an exterior staircase that descended from the bedroom above the former garage which now housed the kitchen.

I fixed Dean a margarita, and she sat on a stool as I cooked Spanish rice. It amused her that she'd had to talk me into adding sautéed onions, grated cheddar cheese, and bacon to the Campbell's recipe on the side of the can. For the time being we did not discuss the paranormal.

After dinner we lay down on the bunk beds that doubled as couches. As if tiptoeing around broken glass we began to discuss the supernatural.

"Pappy is dead," I began, "so your having imagined the pipe smoke wouldn't have summoned his spirit unless we were a mortal match."

Dean defended her independence. "Maybe Pappy is saying we're fine the way we are!"

"You mean, he came back from the dead to warn us *not* to get married?"

A look of resignation came over her. She seemed to have aged suddenly.

"No," she said. "My daughters are miserable. Their friends' mothers are boycotting me and taking it out on the girls. We have to get married. I'm sorry." I was stunned. Was she proposing and apologizing at the same time?

"What do you mean 'have to'?" I said.

"The girls aren't being invited to spend-the-night parties," she said, "because the other mothers don't approve of me." This was a euphemism for *are jealous of me*. Dean's former Ole Miss classmates and sorority sisters were a closed society. At first they celebrated Dean's return to Oxford until her presence at cocktail parties drew too much attention. With slitted eyelids they watched their husbands compete for Dean's approval. Something had to give.

"Being married isn't the same as being in love," she went on. "If I had any sense I'd marry the next man I meet with five hundred thousand in the bank." This pronouncement would have depressed me if I hadn't seen Dean give the bank president the heave-ho.

"Okay, fine!" I said as though entering into a suicide pact. "I'll marry a rich widow, and you and I can meet in Memphis once a year and swap war stories."

The foxhole humor amused her. The existential crisis passed. We relaxed on the bunk beds and fell asleep. It could have been the margaritas.

At one o'clock she nudged me awake. It was time to take Chrissy, the babysitter, home. I volunteered to drop Chrissy off at Rowan Oak, where she was the caretaker. When we arrived at 510 South Lamar, Dean decided she would leave the children unattended long enough to ride with me and Chrissy. Looking back, I wonder if Pappy's ghost had a hand in the decision.

Chrissy lived in the cottage behind the main house. In those days Rowan Oak had no exterior lights, and being afraid of the dark, Chrissy wanted us to escort her to the cottage. We walked up the curving driveway lined by tall cedars.

A silent explosion of light surprised us. Thousands of fireflies simultaneously lit up in the treetops. We stopped in amazement and looked up. Normally fireflies don't all glow at once. One or two flash mating signals and others reply. An eerie phosphorescence clung to the cedars as if the lightning bugs were in league with ghosts.

"Pappy!" Dean scolded.

"Yeah, Mr. William is with us," Chrissy said.

- 8 -

Married with Children

IN SEPTEMBER 1972, DEAN AND I POSTPONED OUR WEDDING to give Diane a hayride. As a child Dean had enjoyed going on hayrides with her uncle William. He'd hitch a horse to a wagon and take his girls and their friends to a deserted pasture on Old Taylor Road. Dean and her friends scavenged for firewood. After they roasted hotdogs he treated them to stories and sometimes an astronomy lesson. Diane's twelfth birthday was the perfect time for Dean to reprise this family tradition.

Billy Ross Brown loaned us an empty cotton trailer for the hayride. As a boy he had gone on Faulkner's hayrides. Colonel William Baker, Faulkner's next-door neighbor, loaned us his Ford pickup. Bearing the precious cargo of Diane and her friends, I towed the cotton trailer at a stately twenty mph as Dean followed in the station wagon with emergency blinkers going. At the Hale farm we entertained the children with a bonfire, hot dogs, games, and stories.

Our wedding did not go as smoothly.

A week before the big event I realized that in rescheduling the wedding Dean had selected October 4, the date of my first marriage. Shocked that I'd neglected to mention the coincidence, Dean changed the wedding date to October 6.

"Let's not push our luck," she said.

We arranged for a justice of the peace to perform a civil ceremony. Cho Cho graciously offered to give the reception. The night before the wedding Dean and I hosted a dinner party at Miss Maud's house. Seated on the Faulkner side of the table were Cho Cho, Vicki, and Louise, who had brought a flask of bourbon. On the Wells side were my parents, Glenn and Dorothy, and my sister, Jane.

Cho Cho and Vicki were at their charming best. Louise tried to light a cigarette with a candle and as usual it fell over. Dean quickly righted the burning candle. My parents and sister looked on in bewilderment. Cho Cho and Vicki could barely suppress their amusement.

Dessert was served in the living room, and Dean failed to notice that Louise had taken Diane and Paige into the front bedroom. Behind the closed door Louise was telling the girls that if their mother married me, she and their father could never be reunited and their lives would be ruined. As we carried dessert trays up the hallway screams of anguish came from the bedroom. Dean excused herself and went to see what was going on.

"Louise seems to have come down with the wedding jitters," I announced to my parents. Vicki and Cho Cho squeezed each other's hand to keep from laughing. I asked my mother to play the piano. As a church organist and piano teacher she had repertoires for any emergency. She began to play "Somewhere over the Rainbow." Cho Cho and Vicki were beside themselves. In the girls' bedroom Jon was playing "Pong" on the TV set. Hearing the piano he went into the living room and asked "Miss Dorothy" to play the theme from the movie, *The Sting*. Without missing a beat my mother began to play the popular tune. By then the girls' sobbing had subsided. Dean emerged from her bedroom and signaled me.

"I'm throwing Louise out," she said. "Take your family to the motel."

"What do I tell them?"

"I don't care. Just get them out of here!"

With Jaybird on the piano bench next to her, Miss Dorothy smoothly modulated into "Love Is a Many Splendored Thing." Unbelievable, I thought. Sometimes I didn't give my mother enough credit.

Once on a high and windy hill
In the morning mist
Two lovers kissed
And the world stood still

Vicki and Cho Cho were in hysterics. When my mother finished playing I apologized for Louise's "not being herself" and hustled Jane and my parents out. We walked to the car in silence. They knew better than to ask.

When I returned, Dean reported that she'd found her daughters hysterical and panic-stricken. They begged her not to marry "Mr. Wells"—which against my wishes Dean had made her children address me. I wanted them to call me "Larry" but being determined to do things Pappy's way and harkening back to the "Old Colonel" and antebellum days, she wanted her children to show respect for their elders. This rule had backfired and caused them to view me as an outsider.

"I told the girls," she went on, "that despite their grandmother's ravings there was no chance I would ever get back together with their father. And come the morrow we were going to be married." The girls retreated to their bedroom. Then Dean demanded an apology from her mother.

"Do you have any more bourbon?" Louise said.

Ironically, if Louise had apologized for her sabotage, Dean, who I believe was beginning to second-guess marrying me, might have postponed the wedding. I had no such doubts but sensed that Dean was wondering if she'd made the right decision. Having overplayed her hand, Louise unwittingly forced her principled daughter to stand by her decision.

Vicki and Cho Cho tried to camp on the battlefield but Dean herded them out. Then she took her confused inebriated mother home and put her to bed. On the way back she decided we would have a private wedding ceremony with no family members present. Diane and Paige would not be allowed to serve as bridesmaids. Neither would Jaybird give his mother away. The only witnesses would be our friends John Davis and Jenny Baldwin. "When the JP asks if anyone objects to the marriage," Dean said, "there will be blessed silence."

On Friday, October 6, we taught our college classes as scheduled. My sophomore literature students asked why I was wearing a coat and tie instead of my usual shirt and slacks.

"I'm getting married," I told them.

Cho Cho gave the wedding reception at her home on St. Andrew's Circle. My father, having appointed himself wedding photographer, prowled with Polaroid in hand. He photographed Dean and me, Vicki and Dean, Louise and Dean, my mother and my mother-in-law, the wedding guests, and The Reverend Alfred (Chip) Marble, our Episcopal priest who had come to bless the marriage. Dean's bewildered children, bless them, made the best of it. Diane even placed a plastic bride and groom on the cake.

Dean's wedding dress was a baby blue sweater dress. She later regretted her choice. "I never wear blue," she said. "We should have jumped the broom." Her mood was growing dark as she and Vicki went outside to smoke.

"Well, at least the hors d'oeuvres are perfect!" Dean broke the silence.

"You'll never repay my mother for the reception," Vicki said abruptly.

"And you'll never repay me for planting your husband," Dean shot back without thinking. The girls of Rowan Oak stepped on their cigarettes, put on fixed smiles, and returned to the reception. To the casual observer such an exchange might reek of bitterness, but not to step-cousins frozen in time while Pappy's lightning crashed around them.

Kate Baker drew Dean and me into Cho Cho's kitchen and began to dance, all five feet one of her. We looked on in wonder. A bit out of breath she explained, "Someone's got to dance at your wedding to give you luck!" We hugged Miss Kate. Her seal of approval represented the town's blessing.

Because of my offhand remark—"I'd like to spend the first night of the honeymoon with a blue neon sign outside my window"—John and Jenny insisted on coordinating the honeymoon. They reserved rooms at a hotel in Vicksburg overlooking the Mississippi River. The lobby had stained carpets that stank of stale cigars. Dean stood by the elevator as I registered. A young woman with heavy makeup approached me.

"I'm here for my honeymoon," I spoke up, indicating my bride waiting with the luggage.

"Well, congratulations!" said the hooker. Thinking Dean would find this amusing I related what had happened.

"You should have hired her to consummate the marriage," Dean said. Some start to our honeymoon! I thought.

"Going up!" said the elevator operator.

The "honeymoon suite" had steam radiators. Outside the window a blue neon light flashed on and off. It looked as if Davis, who would go on to become a successful television and Broadway designer, had dressed the set. We got ready for bed. I switched off the overhead light.

"Our lovely Wednesday nights are over," Dean lamented. "You have ruined a perfectly good affair!" She buried her face in a pillow. The blue neon light blinked mercilessly. I told myself that she was exhausted, that the post-wedding blues would pass. Sure enough, after a while she softened. She was after all still Dean.

At breakfast John announced a change of plans. Instead of proceeding to New Orleans we would detour to Jackson to attend the Ole Miss-Auburn football game. I'd been expecting this announcement, whereas Dean was looking forward to a Bloody Mary in the

French Quarter. The thought of offering her a hotdog at Memorial Stadium worried me. How would she react?

We found seats in the student section. Cheerleaders hurled bundles of miniature rebel flags into the crowd. In those days rebel flags on staffs were used as pom-poms. The university would ban the custom twenty-five years later.

Someone handed Dean a flagstaff. She held it at arm's length in a vengeance-is-mine pose. The band played the national anthem. Everyone stood except for a thick-necked young man seated in front of us. Out of my peripheral vision I saw a flash of red and blue. Dean had smashed the flagstaff over the poor guy's head. Her great-great-grandfather had been a Confederate colonel at the First Battle of Mannassas yet here she was holding the Stars and Bars and singing, "*By the rocket's red glare, the bombs bursting in air.*" The young man turned around seeking revenge. Making like plastic man I stretched my upper torso out of harm's way.

"Gladys," I said to the surprised stranger next to me, "did you want a Sprite or a Coke?"

Dean wore a look of grim satisfaction. She'd saved the honeymoon from being a complete disaster.

- 9 -

The Cofield Collection

HOWARD G. DUVALL JR. WAS COURTING ME. AN OXFORD clothier and Faulkner collector who claimed to have dated Jill Faulkner in high school, Duvall in 1975 founded an independent publishing company which he called Yoknapatawpha Press. At first Dean and I thought it cheeky of Duvall to have hitched his wagon to Faulkner's fictional county. Of all the people we knew, only Howard Duvall, tireless promoter of Faulkner lore and legend, would have appropriated the sacred name.

While clerking at his grandfather's First National Bank in 1919 William Faulkner noticed an obsolete bank account, the Yoknapatawpha Watershed District, named for the Yoknapatawpha Indians, who lived along what is now called the Yocona River. The tribe, which was part of the Chickasaw nation, disappeared somewhere along the Trail of Tears. Bank clerk Faulkner had struck gold. With this Chickasaw name he crowned his fictional county.

Duvall launched his small press by reissuing three of John Faulkner's out-of-print books: *Men Working*, *Dollar Cotton*, and *My Brother, Bill.* He then approached William Faulkner's family photographer, "Colonel" J. R. Cofield, and obtained permission to publish Cofield's Faulkner scrapbook. What Howard didn't tell me, at least not right away, was that he was courting me to edit the Cofield album.

Having discovered that we were fellow members of SAE fraternity (Duvall at Ole Miss and I at the University of Alabama)

Howard invited me to a rush party at the Parks home in Oxford. As I shook hands with freshmen rushees it felt strange to give them the SAE grip when in actuality *I* was the rushee.

The courtship continued as Howard took me to see Lafayette County landmarks associated with Faulkner's work. Having grown up in Oxford and majored in history at Ole Miss, Duvall knew every road, paved and unpaved, and had all but memorized the map Faulkner had drawn of Yoknapatawpha County for the 1946 publication of *The Portable Faulkner*. He'd been an extra in *Intruder in the Dust*, which was filmed in Oxford in 1948, and had been invited to the party Jill Faulkner gave at Rowan Oak for film star Claude Jarman Jr.

Duvall collected anecdotes about people and places associated with Faulkner's work. His two-day tour of Lafayette County helped me recognize these same landmarks later in J. R. Cofield's photograph collection. Howard showed me the iron bridge on the Yocona River, *aka* the Bundren crossing in *As I Lay Dying*, and the original "Reivers Road," a one-hundred-year-old, wheel-rutted trail that Faulkner made famous in *The Reivers*. When Duvall mentioned that he'd bought the farm because the old Reivers road passed through the property I began to think of him as a combination of Faulkner's characters "Will Varner," the shrewd landowner in Frenchman's Bend, and "V. K. Ratliff," the garrulous sewing machine salesman. From then on, the hamlets, cemeteries, and general stores of 1970s Lafayette County existed for me on two levels, real and imaginary. Needless to say, I was grateful to Howard and especially for showing me Faulkner's farm on the eastern edge of Lafayette County, which he claimed was the birthplace of the rapacious, amoral, Mephistophelian "Flem Snopes."

Originally the farm had belonged to Joe Parks. In 1938 Faulkner purchased the property (vengefully, Howard said) after selling movie rights to *The Unvanquished*. He named the farm "Greenfield" and began to raise corn and breed mules.

Dean told me that the Faulkner family's relations soured with Joe Parks in 1920 when he succeeded William's grandfather, J. W. T.

Falkner, as president of the First National Bank of Oxford. (In fairness to Parks, the bank's board of directors voted to retire J. W. T. due to his advanced age. Borrowers had to wait for the "Young Colonel" to finish his afternoon nap before loans could be signed.) But when Parks purchased Murry Falkner's home on North Lamar where William had lived as a teenager, it seemed, at least to Dean and her family, that Joe Parks was on a personal quest to conquer, or outlast, the Faulkner dynasty.

"Pappy avenged his grandfather's ouster," Dean said, "by basing Flem Snopes on Joe Parks. The problem was that unless Joe Parks actually read Pappy, how was he to know he was Flem Snopes?"

When Howard took me to the farm in 1976 the original Parks farmhouse had been uninhabited for nearly two decades. At William Faulkner's death, his daughter Jill inherited the property. She sold it to her cousin, Jimmy Faulkner, who allowed the buildings—house and cabin—to fall into ruin. As I peered through broken windows into shadowy rooms I recalled that Faulkner's working title for *Light in August* was "Dark House." To Faulkner, abandoned farmhouses such as the Parks house represented masked tragedies, their dark, glassless windows empty and misbegotten.

Fifty paces from the main house was a hunting cabin that Faulkner built himself. It, too, was abandoned and deteriorating. Squatters had left litter behind.

"Someone should mention this to Jimmy," I told Duvall, who stared at me in mild surprise.

"*You don't tell a Faulkner what to do!*" he said.

I took this remark as an off-hand compliment. Being married to a Faulkner was not the same as being one.

The farm, which bordered Holly Springs National Forest, was as close to the "Big Woods" as William Faulkner could get. In hunting season he holed up in the cabin for a week at a time. He raised mules on the 320-acre farm, and grew corn. Eventually he moved an African American caretaker into the farmhouse.

Given the attitudes of the time Faulkner knew Joe Parks would not like a black caretaker living next to the Parks family cemetery.

It wasn't long before Joe Parks disinterred his parents' coffins and, in a surreal echo of Addie Bundren's journey in *As I Lay Dying*, transported them to Oxford for reburial. I feel certain that William would have insisted on being present at the disentombment.

I stood on the ridge where the Parks family was once buried and imagined the author leaning on the fence, smoking his pipe, a mule looking over his shoulder. Just then, a wizened vulture lit in a tall pine with an almost-human satisfaction.

In a *Paris Review* interview conducted by Jean Stein, Faulkner famously observed, "If I were reincarnated, I'd want to come back a buzzard. Nothing hates him or envies him or wants him or needs him. He is never bothered or in danger, and he can eat anything."

Over the years every time I visited Greenfield Farm a resident vulture was roosting in the ruins of the farmhouse. Where had I seen that beady stare? At my apartment window?

Hollywood director Jerzy Kromolowski optioned *As I Lay Dying* and was planning to cast Robert Duvall as "Darl" and Marlon Brando as "Dr. Peabody." In the novel Dr. Peabody is so overweight he must be winched up the hill to attend the dying Addie Bundren. At the time Brando's weight made him ideal for the cameo role.

During a visit to Los Angeles, Dean and I invited Kromolowski to have lunch with us and Faulkner's former mistress, Meta Carpenter Wilde. When I told him about the Parks farm and its caretaker buzzard, Jerzy promised to commit part of his film budget to restore the farmhouse as the "Bundren" home. He also offered to donate any period furnishings to the University of Mississippi. When Jill Faulkner Summers died in 2008 Kromolowski was however unable to renew his option. Even then, there still was time to restore the farmhouse, which now sadly is in an irreversible state of collapse.

Before Faulkner's hunting cabin was torched by arsonists, Dean and I visited the farm. She hadn't been there since she and her uncle went deer hunting in 1958. To her the tiny cabin was a shrine. It had a wood-burning stove, a couple of bunk beds, and a tin roof. No electricity or plumbing. I could see them together. Dean sitting on the bunk cleaning her grandfather's rifle. Faulkner reading a newspaper. A light rain falling.

Dean recalled the last time she and her uncle went hunting. They spent the night in the cabin, and before daybreak they climbed into a deer stand Faulkner had made at the edge of Holly Springs National Forest. A better than average shot, she was underequipped that day with a Winchester .218-Bee, her grandfather Sanford Hale's varmint rifle, which lacked the firepower to bring down a deer.

"I wounded a deer," she said with regret. "I tried for a head shot but the bullet struck the shoulder. Pappy was determined to put the poor thing out of its misery. We tracked the blood trail in vain. That was my last deer hunt."

It's a shame that the university neglected to repair the buildings and especially Faulkner's sanctuary, the snug hunting cabin. While the farmhouse was still intact, Dean and I tried to float a restoration project, to no avail. After unknown arsonists burned it she observed, "Well, Pappy would not have wanted scholars poking around. He might even have encouraged the arsonist." All that remains of the hunting cabin today are embers and a few bricks.

J. R. Cofield, whom I met while visiting his photography studio on Jackson Avenue west of the square, died in 1973. His son Jack Cofield succeeded him as chief Ole Miss photographer. Howard approached Jack about publishing the Cofield collection.

Over a thirty-year period, J. R. Cofield photographed Faulkner in his studio using 5 x 7 negatives. The detail of the large negatives was stunning. There were six sittings over three decades. You can see Faulkner aging in them and, if you look again, becoming resigned to his celebrity-hood.

Cofield's first portrait of William Faulkner was a 1931 publicity picture for his novel *Sanctuary*. I chose that photo of Faulkner in tweed jacket, cigarette in hand for the cover of *William Faulkner: The Cofield Collection*.

What was needed to tell the parallel stories of the man and his work were pictures evoking Yoknapatawpha County. I asked Jack Cofield if his father had any old photos of town and county. He took me into a storage space that turned out to be the Yoknapatawpha equivalent of King Tut's tomb. Here were boxes of prints and negatives which Cofield's father had purchased from his predecessors in Oxford, photographers Sanders and Sweeney, whose collection included 5" x 7" negatives of antebellum homes, sharecroppers' cabins, plantations gone to seed, country stores, mule-trading on the town square. In effect Sanders and Sweeney were documenting "Yoknapatawpha" and "Jefferson" before Faulkner was born.

Dean contributed dozens of family pictures and snapshots to the Cofield project. She went to the University of Mississippi Library with me and researched Ole Miss yearbooks for photos of William, Estelle, and Faulkner's classmate and first literary agent, Ben Wasson.

The 1919–1920 yearbooks contained Faulkner's pen-and-ink sketches of social clubs and organizations. Several group photos included the author, then a student.

I put out the word that I needed snapshots of Faulkner. Somehow I heard from Dan Brennan, a former college student from Iowa who'd made a pilgrimage to Rowan Oak in 1940 and happened upon Faulkner writing outdoors under the cedars. Brennan allowed us to publish his candid photographs in *The Cofield Collection.*

J. W. T. Falkner took a photographer along on a road trip to Memphis, c. 1905, to document a rare expedition by automobile. He owned the first car in Oxford, a Buick roadster delivered by rail. And since no one in town knew how to drive a car, Falkner's AfricanAmerican handyman and groom, Chess Carothers, taught himself to start the engine and operate the controls. J. W. T. was the first car owner to drive the eight-hour journey from Oxford to Memphis. The resulting photos show J. W. T. Falkner standing beside his Buick stuck in a suspiciously flooded ditch. Other pictures depicted chauffeur Chess Carothers and farmers at a general store evoking scenes in Faulkner's novel, *The Reivers*.

Cofield's collection included pictures of young William and his brothers at their home and in the studio. One can almost hear the photographer telling them not to move while he ducked under his shroud and removed the lens cover. Dean's private collection included photographs of Faulkner's ancestors, his mother as a bride, a young mother holding her firstborn, William, and portraits of the Faulkner boys at home and at school.

Among Cofield's 5 x 7 negatives I found an image of mule-trading on the square. "Silver Crown," a legendary jackass, was known throughout the county for his bloodline. Faulkner, an inveterate champion of mules, may have been present as a child at this very mule-trading. These documentary photos provide visual evidence that Faulkner did not need to go far afield for characters and settings.

Editing *The Cofield Collection* satisfied something that had been missing in my life. I'd written three unpublished novels and had begun a fourth, but editing allowed me a freedom of expression that I'd never experienced.

Jack Cofield's graduate assistant, Bill Smith, laid out the Cofield book. Every week for several months I drove back and forth to Smith's home near Water Valley to collect the next chapter and show it to Jack and Howard. When lightning struck Miss Maud's house on July 27, 1976, it was the Cofield layout that I grabbed as I fled the fire.

- 10 -

Home Fires Burning

In July of 1976 lightning struck Miss Maud's house and set it on fire. Throughout the ensuing panic Dean was calm and collected, which at the time seemed extraordinary. In retrospect, her composure wasn't surprising. A croquet match in a lightning storm had prepared her.

It was an ordinary weeknight. Dean was cooking dinner for eight including her children and mine, who were then on summer vacation with us—Lawrence, eleven, and Catherine, seven—plus an unexpected house guest, Richard Godden, a British Faulkner scholar. We'd planned to leave the following day for Florida. Jon, ten, and Lawrence were watching TV. Diane, fifteen, and Paige, thirteen, were running hair dryers. Our boxer, Beauregard, banished for trying to steal a chicken leg, was sulking in the backyard. Just before the lightning struck I was showing Richard Godden the original draft of the Cofield album, which I'd spread out on the Absalom table.

The kitchen phone rang and Dean answered. Jon's Little League coach was calling to say that Jon had made the all-star team.

"That's wonderful!" Dean said just as lightning struck the phone line. The receiver in her hand vibrated so violently that it knocked her down. The lights went out. Not Dean's, the house's. The children screamed. Witnesses across the street later told us a bolt of electricity circled the eaves of the house like a blue neon light. Rain came down in sheets. In the dark Dean asked if I was all right. I was not hurt but more startled than the day we got married. Our houseguest, Godden, a serious young man in his twenties, seemed stunned at his good fortune. Faulkner's mother's house was burning and he was there.

Dean lit a candle. The children stormed into the kitchen and latched onto us. We smelled smoke. I ran into the hall, pulled down the folding stairs, and climbed into the attic. Black smoke boiled down into the hallway. I had never been in a house on fire. My feet began moving in place.

"Fire!" I shouted, unnecessarily.

Everybody ran.

Dean rushed across the street to a pay phone and called the fire department. It was raining buckets. I went and got a garden hose, turned on the faucet, bent the hose to shut off the flow (not wanting to make a mess in the house) and dragged the hose into the attic. Godden stood at the foot of the stairs holding a cooking pot filled with water. The smoke in the attic was too thick for me to see the flames. As I retreated down the ladder Dean returned, soaked to the skin, saying that a fire truck was on the way. Lightning and thunder continued like an artillery barrage. The *Oxford Eagle* later reported that thirty-nine recorded lightning strikes occurred over a five-minute period and that eight houses were set on fire. The fire department was going crazy.

What to save?

The children.

We found all five perched on a neighbor's front porch with Beauregard, who had jumped the back fence. It's a high fence and he only jumped it the one time. We counted faces. Did you ever count kids in an emergency? You see them and you don't. Where's what's-his-name?

"Right here, Mama."

We grabbed random possessions while flames licked the attic. Dean took the baked chicken out of the oven. Fire or no fire the children had to eat. As she left the kitchen she took down Nannie's

"Don't Complain, Don't Explain" sign while I boxed up the Cofield photo-layout scattered across the dining room table. Still holding the pot of water Godden followed us from room to room.

It's interesting which possessions one rescues from a fire. Remembering a wooden chest containing rare books, letters, and sketches, I asked Howard Duvall and our neighbor, William Lewis, to put the chest in *William's* car. I was afraid Howard would take them home and go through them. He was obsessed with collecting Faulkner, whereas Lewis, Dean's former classmate, could be trusted not to mess with her collection.

As they carried the chest into the street the two gentlemen got into a tug of war in the middle of South Lamar Boulevard. Howard's car was in the Chevron parking lot and William had parked at the Texaco station across the street. A traffic jam formed as a crowd of spectators watched Neilson's Department Store out-pull Duvall's Men's Shop.

A fire truck pulled up in front of the house. The driver was Larry Brown, later a well-known novelist (*Dirty Work*, *Joe*, *Big Bad Love*). He'd been answering another call when he saw smoke and flames coming from our roof. Luckily for us he stopped in front of our home. Dean's first words to the sagacious Mr. Brown, whom we had never met, were, "What kept you?"

Firemen came and tramped through the house. They switched off power, moved furniture, and accidentally smashed a storm door with a fire hose. A crowd gathered in the yard. Who was the Englishman holding a pot of water? Dean made introductions presenting Godden as a visiting scholar. Our neighbors didn't seem surprised that we had an emergency scholar standing by. Susie James, the *Eagle*'s indefatigable photographer, took Dean's picture next to Paige, hair plastered by rain, clutching the "Don't Complain—Don't Explain" sign. The firemen chopped through a wooden ventilator above the kitchen.

"Set it on spray, Bubba!" one of them yelled.

Our insurance agent Dick Marchbanks sauntered up and remarked, "Go to the motel."

"What, leave home at a time like this?" I said. The next day we realized Marchbanks was informing us that our insurance policy would pay for emergency lodging. By that time Dean had arranged for the children to spend the night with a friend.

The kitchen ceiling was dripping, floors sooty and sopping wet. The firemen set up exhaust fans to suck out the smoke. I gently took Godden's pot away. The crowd broke up just as Dean's cousins arrived. They had heard about the fire and had come to help. Chooky, previously the chief of the volunteer fire department, donned goggles and oxygen tank and climbed into the attic to make sure the fire was out. Jimmy asked if we had anything to drink. In Mississippi, this is known as a disaster party.

We sat in rocking chairs on the gallery, sipped bourbon, and pretended nothing had happened. I thought my in-laws would never leave.

Our British guest helped mop the kitchen. The ceiling was still dripping. The town clock struck two. With nothing else to talk about Godden began an intellectual tirade on capitalism. America was, in general, a materialistic and doomed society, etc. I'm sure he was only trying to distract me but his timing couldn't have been worse. I never thought of myself as a capitalist, but given that our home and its contents had nearly been lost I wished he would shut up. Over the flame of a single candle we got into a shouting match and went to bed without saying goodnight. I, the decadent capitalist, gave our guest the last candle.

The next morning we woke up in a wet, smoky house. The good news was that the house suffered only minor fire damage. The bad news was water damage to ceilings, walls, and floors. Did we want to begin a major cleanup or go to Florida as planned? The children voted to go.

Lightning struck on the twenty-seventh of July. It was Thanksgiving before we set the house straight.

II. Willie Morris and Ole Miss

- 11 -

Willie

WE MET WILLIE MORRIS AT THE 1978 GREENWOOD (MISsissippi) Arts Festival. In his mid-forties, six feet tall, blond, boyish, and brimful of mischief, the former editor-in-chief of *Harper's*, politely shook Vicki's hand and mine, then bowed to Dean, whom our hostess, Mary Jane Whittington, introduced as "Mr. Faulkner's niece." I watched him process the introduction and react to Dean's radiant smile. I'd seen this happen many times. Vicki went looking for someone to talk to. Morris tugged at his collar and suggested we get a cocktail.

"Stand between me and those blue-haired ladies!" he whispered as we went outside. We asked no questions but formed a human barrier between him and a clutch of matrons. It was one of those social emergencies all southerners know well. Morris was in the first pantheon of Mississippi writers alongside William Faulkner, Eudora Welty, Walker Percy, and Shelby Foote. A sixth sense told him when unknown admirers were closing in. "Those ladies will ask me to address their book club," he said. "And I can't say *no* to ladies of my mother's generation."

We didn't know it, but we'd just been tapped as Willie's problem solvers for the coming decade.

As we hovered near the bar Morris said that he was thinking of moving back to Mississippi. In the same breath he asked if we thought he "could stand the pace." Dean observed that she'd had the same concern when she moved from Hilton Head.

"Everybody in Oxford was so nice to me," she went on, "but in Mississippi the problem is that people in your hometown, my old friends and especially my mother's generation, know too much about you."

"*Exactly!*" exclaimed Morris, his eyes lighting up. "Your neighbors feel they can ask you anything." He hesitated, then asked, "Did, uh, Pappy have the same problem?"

I'd seen this happen before. Every writer we met couldn't wait to utter the name "*Pappy*" in Dean's presence.

"Yes!" she readily agreed. "Pappy was obsessed with privacy. He put up a '*Private Yard, PLEASE Do Not Enter' sign* on his gate."

My first impressions of Willie Morris were of his quick reactions, his ability to carry on two conversations at once, an unerring grasp of the core issue, and an ever-present twinkle in his eye. It was as if he took sustenance from the Delta atmosphere and animated conversations around us. His accent grew more southern by the minute.

He plied us with practical questions. How many writers-in-residence did the University of Mississippi have? *None*. How many bars were there in Oxford? *One*. When did the restaurants close? *Ten*. How many restaurants were there? *Four or five*. Was it an expensive place to live? *No*.

"Maybe I wouldn't be put off by the slow pace," he mused, charmed by the idea of a small university town with a single bar and five restaurants—a university without a writer-in-residence.

"Oxford can be pretty quiet," I warned, unaware of how exhilarating the concept of *quiet* is to a former New Yorker accustomed to sirens and car alarms. "The only sounds at midnight are the town clock chiming the hour," I added. In less than a year we'd be sitting in our kitchen with Willie as the courthouse clock chimed twelve times.

Upon learning that we were all staying at the Holiday Inn, he invited us for a nightcap after the arts festival. At 1 a.m. Morris treated us to something that embarrassed us but was apparently routine for him.

"Let's call Bill Styron and wake him up!" he said. Dean and I nursed our nightcaps in dubious silence as he dialed William Styron's home, the time in Connecticut being two a.m. Whom else did we know who could wake up William Styron and get away with it? Whom else did we know who had Styron's unlisted phone number? "Hey, Stingo," Morris said. "William Faulkner's niece wants to talk to you. Her name is Dean."

Dean warily accepted the receiver and after apologizing profusely managed to carry on an awkward conversation. Morris looked on, arms crossed, severely pleased. Writers trust their first impressions. If they like you they are your friend for life. That's how it was for Willie and also, as it turned out, Bill Styron. That night in Greenwood when we sat up swapping tales of misspent youth was, I think, when Willie made up his mind to move to Oxford.

"I'm interested in teaching at Ole Miss," he told us. "Please give the chancellor my regards, will you, Deanie?"

Back in Oxford we made an appointment to see Dr. Porter Fortune, chancellor of the University of Mississippi. When we informed him of Morris's proposal, Fortune was ecstatic. Ole Miss had never had a writer-in-residence. Faulkner had turned them down. The acting English department chair, Evans Harrington, a published novelist, offered a tutorial in creative writing, but there was no writing class, per se.

Dr. Fortune suggested that we work out the details with Robert Khayat, vice chancellor for university affairs. Khayat invited Dr. Ann Abadie of the Center for the Study of Southern Culture to the meeting which took place several days later. Dean sent me as her proxy. Neither of these gifted administrators arrived at work expecting to deal with an unfunded, unprecedented faculty position. From their noncommittal expressions I guessed that they were concerned not just about the salary, which would prove a major hurdle, but how the university would be affected. Morris wasn't an academician nor did he have teaching experience. Why would a successful editor give up the bustle of New York for a small state university? Could he connect with the students? Would he keep regular office hours, grade papers, post final grades? How would he get along with town and gown?

I hadn't considered Morris's motivations. Did he feel burned out? Did he feel that returning to Mississippi would give him a fresh start? Khayat pointed out that the faculty budget for 1979 was already committed. There was no money for a writer-in-residence. This was my administrative baptism under fire. I shrank two shirt sizes. I'd always known liberal arts was an orphan but until then had not experienced the phenomenon.

Khayat referred me to Rufus Jones, head of development. I knew Jones by reputation as a politically savvy fundraiser. Evans Harrington and Ann Abadie also attended the meeting. Harrington, bless him, assured Jones that the English department would be honored to invite Willie to join the faculty. Wearing a poker face, Jones politely listened. Doubtless he'd fielded similar alumni requests to hire a guest lecturer. I had to up the ante.

I told Jones about Morris's plan to invite authors William Styron, George Plimpton, and John Knowles to speak on campus. According to Willie they would come for expenses, I said. My assurances met with dubious glances: The notion that Morris would come and teach at Ole Miss and that his friends would show up *gratis* was pie in the sky.

"If the university pays for lodging," mused Jones, "will those authors take care of room service and restaurant tabs?"

Without thinking I mumbled, "What's the matter, are you afraid Willie will pull it off?"

Fortunately, Jones took my ill manners in stride. No doubt he'd dealt with similar well-meaning alumni who were beyond their depth. To my surprise he acquiesced, up to a point.

"I need to be kept informed," he said, "but please leave my major donors alone. They'll give you a thousand in place of the ten thousand they were planning to give me."

Dean and I had no experience in soliciting donations. She recommended we begin with the First National Bank of Oxford, where her great-grandfather had been founding president and where William at nineteen had worked as teller. When Joe Parks replaced J. W. T. Falkner as bank president, Falkner withdrew his savings of $30,000 from First National, ceremoniously crossed the square with money bags in a wheelbarrow, and opened an account at the Bank of Oxford. His intention was to leave First National without operating funds for a day or two.

We had no idea if the modern-day FNB president knew of J. W. T.'s ouster, but he graciously pledged $2,000. Across the square to the Bank of Oxford we went, Dean and I, just as J. W. T. had done more than half a century ago. Twenty minutes later we had a matching pledge.

Donations from other banks followed, a thousand here, a thousand there. Mississippi Chemical Corporation of Yazoo City, Willie's hometown, was especially generous. We hosted private fundraising parties at our home. Addressing twenty or more guests I pitched Willie as writer-in-residence, listed his achievements, and all but compared him to a comet landing in front of the Lyceum.

A hush came over the room. No one volunteered a donation. Didn't they understand what it would mean to bring Willie Morris to the university? I had assumed I was preaching to the choir.

"What are you getting out of this?" demanded an older gentleman. I was shocked at the implication.

"This is a personal favor to Willie," I replied, implying in my zeal that Morris and I were longtime friends while asking myself why, indeed, were we going to bat for Willie? He'd blown our minds by inviting us into his world. Had we changed existentially in those first few hours with Willie? Our interest of course was altruistic. Yet how could we know that a year hence Morris would ask us to reprint his children's book, *Good Old Boy: A Delta Boyhood*, which Yoknapatawpha Press would keep in print to this very day or that we'd bring *North Toward Home* back into print and publish three other books by Morris. That night in Greenwood, we'd connected as believers in the written word, yet on a deeper level had our collective sensibilities—Dean's and mine—recognized opportunity knocking at the door?

"Anyone who has read and appreciated *North Toward Home*," I added, "would be gratified to help bring its author home to Mississippi. Dean and I are honored that Willie asked us to represent him."

We raised several thousand dollars that evening. Aided by a $7,000 pledge by Will Norton, chair of the journalism department, we were able to fund Morris's first year of teaching beginning in January 1980. It was unprecedented for one university department to fund a salary for another, but Norton had his eyes on the horizon. After his first year at Ole Miss, Willie would leave the English department for journalism.

- 12 -

Willie's Scouting Trip

DUKE UNIVERSITY, WE HEARD LATER, HAD OFFERED MORRIS twice as much as Ole Miss, but North Carolina wasn't where he wanted to be. As he liked to say, "I always wanted to come back to Mississippi but not in a pine box."

We wrote Morris that his salary had been guaranteed. He didn't respond right away. It wasn't Duke's offer that gave him pause. He wanted to scout Oxford and Ole Miss before he made up his mind.

To cover his travel expenses we contacted Sid Graves, our fellow graduate student, director of the Carnegie Library in Clarksdale, and cofounder of the Delta Museum. Graves was delighted at the opportunity of having Morris appear at the Carnegie Library. The Carnegie budget allowed for two speakers per annum at $250 per speaker. Sid combined his total promotions budget to pay Morris's airfare, lodging, and rental car expenses. We agreed to attend the Clarksdale event and escort Morris to Oxford.

Accompanied by Adam Shaw, son of the novelist Irwin Shaw, Morris flew to Jackson. They spent the night in Yazoo City, where Morris's friends gave him a welcoming party. At the Carnegie Library he read to an enthusiastic audience from *North Toward Home*.

After the program, Dean rode to Oxford with Adam Shaw, and Morris rode with me. He tuned the radio to the World Series of 1979. Willie Stargell and the Pittsburg Pirates were playing Baltimore. This was the first of many nights with Willie listening to games on the radio. He mused that he could have gone into sports broadcasting. Roone Arledge once offered him a job with ABC.

"I was tempted," he said, "but I couldn't sacrifice my writing."

We drove the straight roads of the Delta listening to the World Series. The flatlands were ghostly in the gloom, farmhouses like tiny islands of light. Baseball and cotton. Willie Morris was where he belonged.

Willie and I discovered that we had a lot in common. At an early age we both began to write about our experiences. At thirteen he was writing a school column for the *Yazoo City Herald*. At ten I won a 4-H Club essay contest in Ozark, Alabama. We were both high school band members, and as trumpet players we both played "Taps" at military funerals of Korean War dead. Our mothers were piano teachers and church organists.

As we spoke of Faulkner's Mississippi the headlights illuminated cotton trailers parked alongside the road. When Willie asked if we could visit Rowan Oak I readily agreed. Dean and I hadn't planned to stop there, but I knew that she would enjoy showing Rowan Oak to Willie. Doubtless as we turned off on Old Taylor Road she was informing Adam where we were headed. At Rowan Oak the house and grounds were closed for the night, but that was no problem.

"If the university police show up Dean will vouch for us," I told Willie.

"Maybe they'll join us for a toast to Mr. Bill," he joked.

The four of us walked up the dark, curving driveway, the house a spectral white under a full moon. Morris took a pint of Jack Daniel's from his pocket. Passing the bottle, we toasted Dean's uncle beneath the cedars.

The next night, a tumultuous Friday on a football weekend in good weather, we hosted a cocktail party at Miss Maud's. Donors who'd contributed to Willie's salary fund gave him a warm welcome. He loved meeting our friends.

"These are good people," Adam Shaw told Willie. "You'd be crazy not to come here."

Afterward we had dinner at Taylor Grocery, a combination catfish restaurant and country store located six miles south of Oxford. Morris gazed in delight at the gas pumps in front of the store. We could smell catfish frying. Judging by Morris's expression one might think we'd taken him to Four Seasons South.

"Don't worry, no reservations needed," I told him.

Willie was familiar with Taylor as a setting in the novel *Sanctuary* but had assumed it was a fictional place. Armed with facts from Howard Duvall's "Yoknapatawpha" tour I told him that before the Civil War the Yocona River bottomland around Taylor produced so much cotton that a shallow draft paddleboat was needed to haul the bales to Natchez. Dean broke in to tell Morris and our other guests, who included artist Bill Dunlap and Senator Thad Cochran, how, in 1942, she, Jill, and Vicki had run away from home in cart-and-pony and gone to Taylor.

"We drank water from a gourd dipped in the watering trough in front of Taylor Grocery," she said. "Pappy had the sheriff's department searching for us."

To Willie, and especially to Dunlap, the interior walls of the café begged for inscriptions. With owner Mary Katherine Hudson's permission, Dunlap sketched a crop duster flying low over cotton fields, a Delta horizon covering an entire wall. Thad Cochran added an inscription, then gave Willie the magic marker.

"This is where Faulkner's Temple Drake and Gowan Stevens got off the train looking for a bootlegger," he wrote and signed his name with a flourish.

The next time we went to Taylor Grocery, the walls were completely covered with Bobby-loves-Sally graffiti. I tried in vain to find Dunlap's crop-duster mural and the inscriptions by Morris and Cochran.

Willie's introduction to Oxford wouldn't have been complete without a tailgate party. That weekend Ole Miss was playing Georgia. We took him to the Grove, ten acres of trees, grass, and shade on the Ole Miss campus. During football season the Grove was "old home week" for alumni and students. In those days football fans parked under the oaks. Typically on game day you'd see fifty tailgating parties whereas today they number well over a thousand.

Our tailgate served up the usual Bloody Marys and fried chicken, but to Morris it was the conversation that mattered. These Oxford natives had grown up calling William Faulkner "Pappy," but more importantly they had grown up in Faulkner's Oxford. They kept ponies in their grandfathers' barns. They witnessed mule-trading on the square. With an intimate knowledge of settings and characters in Faulkner's stories they spoke of his fiction as if it had happened yesterday. Like characters in *The Mansion* or *Light in August* they interrupted each other's stories with observations or corrections as if they had absorbed Faulkner's writings at birth. For Willie's benefit one of the hosts burlesqued, "*If you're thinking about calling me a Snopes do it to my face!*"

Enrapt, drink in hand, Willie listened to an anecdote on his left while eavesdropping on a conversation on his right. People dropped by our tailgate to welcome him to Ole Miss. Having failed to support William Faulkner in the manner he deserved, the townspeople made up for this collective omission by lavishing affection on Morris, who, let's face it, was easier to love.

That Saturday in October, surrounded by kindred spirits, Morris told us goodbye with a cheerful wave, saying, "See you New Year's Eve!"

- 13 -

16 Faculty Row

A week before Christmas it occurred to me to check on Morris's housing reservation. The chancellor's secretary informed me that no faculty house had been secured, and to her knowledge Morris hadn't requested one. She suggested I contact Dr. Charles Noyes, vice chancellor in charge of university affairs.

When I attended graduate school at Ole Miss, Dr. Noyes was one of my favorite English professors. His specialty was a blend of literature and contemporary history. With Noyes you didn't just study Restoration drama but went backstage and hobnobbed with actors and playwrights. Sitting cross-legged on his desk, grinning slyly, his chin resting on his knuckles, Noyes delivered an entertaining account of the period.

At a cocktail party Vicki gave for graduate students—she was completing a master's degree in modern languages—we began impersonating our favorite professors. I imitated Noyes. Sitting cross-legged on a table, waggling my head in a satisfied way, I gossiped about backstage affairs in Congreve's day. Everyone seemed to enjoy my little act. What I didn't know was that one of the smiling faces belonged to a twenty-five-year-old assistant professor. Word soon got around.

The minute I poked my head into the vice chancellor's office I could tell by Noyes's expression that he had not forgotten my student parody. I could only hope that for Morris's benefit and that of the university Noyes would put aside slights real or imagined. He listened in stony silence as I inquired about a faculty house for Morris.

"I have assigned the last vacancy to a freshman law student," he replied, prim and officious. "He is to pick up the keys to 16 Faculty Row this afternoon." He dangled the keys before my eyes. I began apologizing for bringing up Morris's housing at the ninth hour.

"Could the law student possibly be assigned an apartment in married student housing?" I asked. Vice Chancellor Noyes crossed his arms.

I left his office, walked down the Lyceum corridor, and knocked on the chancellor's door. In those days if you were lucky you could see the chancellor without an appointment. Dr. Fortune kindly made time for me and expressed his delight that Morris was coming. When I brought up housing, he said that someone on his staff would take care of it. I felt I had no choice but to mention the "still-available" 16 Faculty Row. Fortune gestured at the door. I stepped into the corridor. Glowing with anticipation is a cliché but there you have it. After a moment the chancellor came to the door.

"Go check with Dr. Noyes," he said.

I found Noyes holding out the keys to 16 Faculty Row, his gaze averted. Manners belatedly kicked in.

"I hope I'm not inconveniencing anyone," I said.

"I do what the chancellor tells me," Noyes replied in a monotone, staring at the wall over my head. Later I heard that Noyes had been one of two English faculty members who voted against inviting Morris to join their staff.

The reason? Willie lacked a PhD.

Dean and I couldn't wait to inspect 16 Faculty Row. The two-bedroom 1930s-era cottage had been built by the WPA. The living room opened on the dining room. There was a small kitchen and a single bathroom. The house was in great shape but unfurnished.

Dean and her Willie-Altar-Guild (WAG) sprang into action. They began by renting two double beds, a Danish-style sofa, and various chairs including an easy chair that resembled Faulkner's favorite chair at Rowan Oak. Sarah Davidson, an antique dealer, provided an unfinished dining room set and some paintings. I noticed the unfinished table and asked if she needed it returned in mint condition. She observed that if Willie "distressed" the surface it would be fine with her. The table would be in demand as a collectible.

The women collected bed linens, towels, pictures, vases, and ashtrays. They made up beds, filled ice trays, and stocked the fridge with milk, doughnuts, and coffee. Using firewood left behind by the previous tenant I laid a fire in the fireplace. The *piece de resistance* was a fifth of Jack Daniel's on the dining room table.

On New Year's Eve Willie and his son David Rae came rolling in. They'd driven in tandem from Long Island, cars crammed with Willie's belongings. David, twenty, was a student at Hampshire College in Amherst. Willie liked pointing out that David had been born on a star-crossed Halloween night in 1959 when LSU's Billy Cannon scored on a punt return to beat Ole Miss.

Willie was charmed with his new home. We let him assume that the university provided the furnishings. A month later he called to report a problem.

"The university billed me for four hundred in rent," he complained, "and a Johnson Furniture Company says I owe forty-five dollars for furniture rental?"

- 14 -

Willie Delivers

At Morris's inaugural lecture students could be seen running to the lecture hall. There was a sportive, holiday air, the kind of anticipation I had only observed at a Bob Dylan concert at Tad Smith Coliseum. Law student John Grisham was among two hundred students and faculty who flocked to that first lecture. Bishop Hall Auditorium was filled to capacity. Professors squatted in the aisles as Willie took the stage. His black Labrador, Pete, slumped beside the podium. Man and dog received a standing ovation. We were witnessing the beginning of a new era at the University of Mississippi.

Faulkner by contrast had given a single lecture in 1947. He'd cautiously agreed to address an English class on condition that no reporters would be present. Unbeknownst to the professor, a student reporter who was a stringer for the Associated Press attended the class. Asked about America's top contemporary authors, Faulkner, believing he was speaking off the record, listed himself along with Thomas Wolfe, John Dos Passos, Ernest Hemingway, and John Steinbeck. When asked his opinion of Hemingway, he joked that "Papa" avoided using words readers had to look up in a dictionary.

The next day in Havana, Hemingway read the AP headline in disbelief. *Faulkner Dice Que Hemingway No Tiene Coraje.* "Faulkner Says Hemingway Lacks Courage." Furious, Hemingway asked a

Yoknapatawpha Press, Inc.
P. O. Box 248, 102½ S. Lamar
Oxford, Mississippi 38655

(601) 234-0909
(601) 234-2419

Lawrence Wells
Director

brigadier-general to write a letter to Faulkner attesting to his courage under fire during World War II.

That was Faulkner's last lecture at Ole Miss.

In his opening remarks Morris thanked university officials. Then he expressed appreciation to "the lovely and brilliant Dean Faulkner Wells, niece of William Faulkner" and her husband, "the distinguished director of Yoknapatawpha Press."

Did he say distinguished? I thought you couldn't be considered distinguished before the age of fifty. I had been wondering about my official title. Publisher, director, editor, janitor.

Pleased to see students taking notes, Morris assigned a reading list of six novels written by friends living and dead beginning with *From Here to Eternity*. He reminisced about writing his memoir *James Jones: A Friendship*. Jones died in 1977 before finishing *Whistle*, the third novel in a trilogy beginning with *From Here to Eternity*. Honoring Jones's deathbed request, Morris completed the novel for his friend. His seamless conclusion was acclaimed by critics and readers. Midway through the lecture Morris looked into the audience.

"Dean Faulkner Wells," he called, "where are you?" Dean raised her hand. Willie continued, whimsical and mischievous, "Censors deleted four-letter words in the first edition of *From Here to Eternity*. What are your thoughts?"

Without hesitation Dean responded that this was how soldiers talked, that in bowdlerizing the novel censors had done Jones an injustice. Willie pounced on the word and asked if any of the students could define *bowdlerizing*. I think that moment defined his transition from lecturer to teacher.

Relaxing afterward, he told us, a little amazed at his transformation, that he felt privileged to be teaching at Ole Miss. As an editor he'd shaped careers and pushed staff writers such as David Halbersham and Larry L. King to new levels. Now he'd entered a new phase in his life.

And the writers came—for expenses only, as Willie had promised—Styron, Plimpton, Knowles, Groom, and Gloria Jones.

Willie began the semester teaching Plimpton's *Paper Lion* and Groom's *Better Times Than These*. Equal time was allotted to festivities. William and Patty Lewis gave a formal dinner party welcoming Winston Groom and George Ames Plimpton. Willie dreamed up an equally elaborate entertainment. Around the dinner table all of us except Plimpton knew what was about to happen.

In 1868 Plimpton's great-grandfather, Adelbert Ames, was the provisional governor of Mississippi. A liberal Republican, Governor Ames advanced the rights of former slaves by appointing blacks to state office. Confederate sympathizers reviled him as "Beast Ames." It had long amused Plimpton and Morris that Willie's great-grandfather, a Confederate colonel and Mississippi legislator, had brought impeachment charges against Adelbert Ames.

Willie talked the sitting Mississippi governor, William Winter, a close personal friend, into issuing a fake proclamation giving Plimpton safe passage out of the state of Mississippi. His offense: being descended from Adelbert P. Ames. Willie read aloud the document drafted in Jackson on the governor's stationery and delivered to him by courier.

Dear Mr. Plimpton,

You are an honored guest today at our State University. Your literary and editorial genius is notable. Your athletic talent has encouraged you to play quarterback, throw baseballs, drive racing cars, box against champions, and slam cymbals together in the symphony orchestra. Your comradeship with our southern writers in New York City, where you so graciously keep them out of trouble, has helped bring the Grand Ole Union back together again.

As governor of Mississippi, I hearwith extend a pardon to your great-grandfather, Adelbert P. Ames, the Republican Reconstructionist governor of our beloved state, and present a document of safe conduct through the ghost of old enemy lines. I pledge that you shall remain free and unmolested in the Sovereign State of Mississippi for 12 hours, beginning at 9:45 AM today, February 26, 1980, ending at 9:45 PM on that day when I understand that your plane departs north from Memphis. I cannot, however, speak for the governor of Tennessee on this matter.

With all best wishes from the people of Mississippi I am sincerely yours,

William F. Winter
Governor

With a blank, poker-faced expression Plimpton listened to Willie read the governor's proclamation. Then University of Mississippi police chief Michael Stewart appeared in the dining room with unloaded pistol pointed at the floor.

"Which of you gentlemen is Mr. George Plimpton?" he demanded. George glanced at Willie, who stared at the ceiling. "On the orders of the governor of Mississippi," Stewart went on, "I am to escort you, sir, to the edge of town where you will be driven to Memphis and placed on an airplane for New York. Mr. Plimpton, if you are ready, please come with me, sir."

Plimpton thanked his hosts, bid good night to his fellow dinner guests, and warned Morris of a swift and terrible retribution. We applauded as Plimpton, accompanied by Stewart and Winston Groom, departed. Later Groom, who had offered to drive Plimpton to Memphis Airport, reported that two patrol cars, blue lights blazing, had escorted his car to the county line at speeds exceeding ninety miles an hour.

"I didn't write that proclamation," Governor Winter protested years later. "Willie wrote it! All I did was have it typed on official stationery. You know, we would do anything for Willie. If we didn't he might renounce our friendship!"

Throughout the spring of 1980 Oxford was treated to the public appearances of writers and sports figures at Willie's invitation. This casual acceptance of celebrity—the "Willie Syndrome" we called it—spread through the town like a virus. By the end of the semester Dean and I were shamelessly dropping the names of America's best-known authors.

Meanwhile, Willie sat in on poker games, drank moonshine, arranged dinner parties, and hung out at the Holiday Inn bar with students and alumni. One evening at the Holiday Inn I introduced him to Oxford's mayor, John Leslie. Morris casually remarked that the mayor of Bridgehampton was waiting in his car. Willie had dubbed his dog Pete "the mayor of Bridgehampton." Bars in Bridgehampton allowed pets, and Pete was a bar dog if ever there was one.

"Why did you leave him in the car?" asked Leslie.

"Well, sir, he's black," Willie said with a straight face. Mayor Leslie was horrified.

"We've put those days behind us!" he declared. "Oxford is a liberal community, and injustice is not tolerated. Let me welcome the mayor of Bridgehampton!" Leslie was on his way to the parking lot when Morris stopped him.

Willie had earned the right to joke about Mississippi's racist past. In his book *Yazoo: The Integration of a Deep Southern Town* he'd addressed how public schools in Yazoo City peacefully integrated in 1971. "I did not want to go back," he wrote. "I finally went home because the urge to be there during its most critical moment was too elemental to resist, and because I would've been ashamed of myself if I had not."

By the time *Yazoo* was published, however, white flight from the public schools was well underway. A year after integration Yazoo City schools were only 40 percent white. White seg-academies sprang into being. In 1980 the population of Oxford, arguably the most liberal town in Mississippi, was two-thirds white. A diverse population of professors and students formed a core of liberalism that ended at the city limits. The county was dry and rural white voters overwhelmingly conservative.

Morris's *North Toward Home*, published in 1967, expressed his belief that white southerners of conscience must judge African Americans by their character, not the color of their skin. Overnight he became a spokesperson for his generation and for a decade or more Willie's autobiography written at the tender age of thirty-two was a secular bible of change.

When Morris arrived in Oxford in 1980 a white backlash to integration was taking place. A private high school academy catering to mostly white students had recently opened. Morris's liberal voice and presence was essential to help keep the state from backsliding into a racist past. To town and gown he was the living embodiment of change.

That said, it was best not to match the living embodiment drink for drink. Bourbon before dinner, wine with meals, Irish coffee after dinner, Black Russians till dawn.

"Pappy liked his liquor, too," Dean observed, "but compared to Willie he was a lightweight." We joke about it now, but Willie's weekend indulgences often extended through Monday and sometimes Tuesday. Between midnight and dawn he could empty a fifth of Jack Daniel's and still be talking when the sun came up.

When he wasn't working on a book he spent half the day phoning friends and setting up dinner parties, preferably at their homes.

Most people had answering machines but Willie used his own caller-ID code. To get him to answer the phone the caller had to hang up after the second ring and redial immediately. It was a rudimentary but effective means of avoiding book club ladies.

Willie went through any number of friends who dared to drink with him. One wife threatened to divorce her husband if he didn't stop hanging out at 16 Faculty Row. Two or three of his drinking buddies received DUI's. Everyone wanted to party with Willie but only the hardiest survived.

In 1980 Oxford had two bars, the Holiday Inn and the Warehouse. The Gin Company opened a year later. At last call, Willie invited everyone in the bar within earshot to come home with him. Bachelors were inclined to accept. Wives took husbands into custody. I think this is a fair summation of the holiday glow Willie cast over the town.

But every glow has its shadow.

- 15 -

Bridgehampton

At the end of Morris's first semester in May 1980, he invited Dean and me to Gloria Jones's annual Memorial Day party on Long Island. "Gloria's bash" was an East End tradition which she and her late husband, James Jones, began in the 1970s.

We drove to New York with Willie in his mother's old white Plymouth sedan. The fenders sported many dents and the interior had never been cleaned. The engine however ran fine. The traveling mayor of Bridgehampton, Pete, shared the backseat with Dean, who ducked every time Willie flicked ashes out the driver's window. As usual she didn't complain. By the time we arrived in Virginia her white linen blazer was charcoal gray.

Willie headed for Harper's Ferry. His interest in going there was not, however, John Brown or the Civil War. He wanted to claim kinship with the Harper family. We arrived on a Sunday evening. Shops had closed. Up and down the streets went Willie until he located a gift shop bearing the name Harper. He beat on the door until a man appeared at an upstairs window.

"We're closed, what do you want?" he called irritably.

Hopeful and sly Morris said, "I'm kin to the Harpers!"

"So what, I'm a Harper, too!" The irate shop owner slammed the window shut. We'd driven two hundred miles out of our way to enact a scene with which Morris could dine out in Bridgehampton.

"Let's go," he said.

Our next stop was Gettysburg, whose attraction for Morris was equally idiosyncratic. He knew the facts about the Battle of Gettysburg, how two great armies had clashed in a decisive engagement which was a turning point in the Civil War, but what interested him was Mississippi's part in the battle.

Set on a low rise looking over the southern end of the park, the state's memorial was the site of the Mississippi brigade's fatal charge. Staring across the field at the distant tree-shadowed ridge Willie was reliving the battle in his mind.

"Go, you Mississippi!" he said echoing the last known words of General William Barksdale, commander of the Mississippi brigade. We viewed the battlefield with the mixed emotions of white southerners. We regretted that our ancestors were on the wrong side of the war but couldn't help feeling a gravitational pull of blood. Gripped by a mutual ambivalence, the three of us turned and regarded the Mississippi Memorial statue.

"Does he look like Archie Manning to you?" Dean said. The statue was that of a young, bareheaded soldier with arm outstretched.

"*Yes!*" cried Willie as if the profound juxtaposed with the ordinary was a Mississippi trademark. "I don't think the similarity is accidental, do you? Heroes are heroes no matter what battles they may fight."

"Well, football after all is a metaphor for war," I remarked. This, I feel certain, was when I conceived the idea for my novel *Let the Band Play Dixie*, about a North/South all-star football game played at Gettysburg in 1896.

In Manhattan Willie dropped us off on West 69th Street where we planned to spend the night with our friends, John and Jenny, whom we'd invited to accompany us to Bridgehampton the next day.

"I'm having lunch with my agent, Sterling Lord," Willie said rather grandly.

"Hey, Sterling is my agent, too!" Dean laughed.

This was the first time we experienced Willie's New York persona, distant, self-absorbed, beyond the reach of ordinary people. It never occurred to us that returning to Bridgehampton would evoke the "other Willie," the editor-in-chief of *Harper's* whom we'd not known, then, but whose agitation and restlessness were well known to us. Perhaps this duality, for want of a better term, in which you could take the man out of the city but you couldn't take the city out of the man, was what kept him up every night—reading, editing, writing, watching movies on television, phoning friends, playing practical jokes.

Bridgehampton had been Willie's first stop on his journey back to Mississippi. After living in the "Cave," as he called Manhattan, the Hamptons allowed him to reconnect with the seasons. The flat potato fields stretching to the horizon reminded him of Yazoo City's cotton fields. He enjoyed exploring Long Island's historic cemeteries, many dating to the seventeenth century. He rode the farm-to-market roads and fell in with hard-drinking Irish and Dutch farmers and tradesmen. He made loyal friends in the Hamptons, not just the Joneses but Bobby and Marina Van, Johnny Angel, and Billy Depetris, owner of the Triple Crown bar, which along with Bobby Van's was Morris's favorite Bridgehampton bar. Depetris had named it in honor of local hero, Carl Yastrzemski. But ten years later Morris's love affair with the Hamptons faded, and he began to think of returning to his native state.

What was the reason for the sudden appearance of his New York persona? Was he having second thoughts about moving to Mississippi?

When we arrived in Bridgehampton with John and Jenny, intermittent squalls were blowing in from the Atlantic. Gulls flew over Main Street. I called Dean's attention to a handwritten sign on a shop window: "Back in Five Minutes." We could have been in Oxford except for the bumper-to-bumper Memorial Day traffic.

At his restaurant owner Bobby Van greeted us and offered a thumbnail history of the saloon. "In the '60s when I first moved out here," he said, "we were all running away from something. I had come back from Vietnam and was starting my life over. Willie Morris had left *Harper's*. Jim Jones was looking for a home in the country, for privacy. In a sense we all had something in common."

We were all running away from something. In 1971 Willie had resigned at *Harper's* and was seeking a new direction. Over the bar counter, framed photos of writers attested to Bobby Van's heyday as a literary Camelot. Dean and I looked at Jill Krementz's famous photo of James Jones, Truman Capote, Willie Morris, and John Knowles—young and confident and a bit self-conscious at having their picture taken.

"It just happened one day," Van said of the photo. "The writers seemed amused that anyone would want to take their picture. They came out in front of the place and stood around laughing while Jill Krementz, the photographer, lay down in the street to get the sign over the building in the picture with them. I stopped traffic so she could get the shot."

Bobby Van was born into the arts. His great-great-aunt was the second wife of poet Walt Whitman. A piano prodigy he was admitted to Julliard at age fifteen. Vietnam interrupted and subsequently derailed his musical career and he opened a bar in Bridgehampton. It was not long before he had a successful business. His number-one patron, Willie Morris, was inspired to write an op-ed piece about Bobby Van's being a hangout for writers and how the potato fields of eastern Long Island reminded him of the Mississippi Delta. The day after the article appeared in the *New York Times* Sunday edition in March of 1973 hundreds of curiosity seekers converged on Bridgehampton.

"We opened in May of '69 and by '72 had a good business," Van recalled as we stood at the bar counter. "New York had not discovered this place yet. This place [Bobby Van's] was like a living room where everyone was welcome. I'd play the piano and the writers could relax. It was a salon—if you'd like to call it that. There was never any hype about the writers who hung out here. Then Willie Morris wrote that op-ed piece for the *New York Times*. The next day it was pandemonium. People were pushing to get inside the place. We had to lock the doors during regular hours. People were wild to get in, and it wasn't for the bluefish. Until Willie's editorial, people had mainly looked at the Hamptons as a seasonal place, a resort area; but not realizing that there was life here year round, creative people they could get along with. That was what attracted the writers. And so the perception changed."

On the eve of Memorial Day, Gloria Jones gave a warm-up party at her home which her late husband, James Jones, had named Chateau Spud.

"What will your friends in the Hamptons think of us?" Dean asked Willie on the way there.

"Don't worry, they are going to love you!" he replied.

In Gloria's kitchen we reconnected with John Knowles, who'd spoken to Willie's class at Ole Miss, and met authors Shana Alexander and John Marquand Jr. Then novelist Irwin Shaw entered by the kitchen door and the atmosphere changed from convivial to electric. The "old lion," as Willie called Shaw, author of *The Young Lions* and *Rich Man, Poor Man*, was the senior novelist in the Hamptons. Soon, songwriters Adolph Green and Betty Comden arrived, and before long Adolph was humming the song we were all thinking about. Comden joined in, and the two of them danced a soft-shoe routine while the rest of us sang along.

Don't make a brand-new start of it, in old New York
You always make it there, you make it anywhere,
It's up to you, New York, New York.

The moment was spontaneous and intense, which sums up the time we spent in the Hamptons. For us it was a busman's holiday in the presence of greatness.

We took our friends John and Jenny to another Memorial Day warm-up party at George and Freddie Plimpton's. Half an hour later the three of us were on Plimpton's deck singing "Are You from

Dixie" to Terry Southern, who'd written a 1961 *Esquire* article about baton twirling at Ole Miss. He seemed to enjoy the song and the sentiment behind it.

Are you from Dixie?
I said from Dixie.
Where the fields of cotton beckon to me.
I'm glad to see you.
Tell me how be you
And the friends I am longing to see.
If you are from Alabama, Tennessee or Caroline
Any place below the Mason Dixon line
Then you're from Dixie.
Hooray for Dixie
Cause I'm from Dixie too!

"You *m-must* sing that at Gloria's bash tomorrow," cried Willie, talent scout for all things southern. "Promise me you will sing it!"

At Chateau Spud the following day Dean and I mingled with such luminaries as US senator Jacob Javits, actor Richard Widmark, and John Lindsay, the former mayor of New York City. Dean met Lauren Bacall, who observed, "You and I were in a film together. . . ." She was referring to Mississippi ETV's *William Faulkner: A Life on Paper*, an award-winning PBS documentary in which Dean and Bacall had been separately interviewed. I stood marveling at my wife as she chatted with Bacall. Here was Pappy's girl in action, unintimidated by a legendary movie star. She chatted with Bacall as if they were old pals. If the Hampton gliterati chose to identify her solely as Faulkner's niece, they had earned the right to do so. This was one of those times when Pappy's shadow lay easy on the skin.

Men carried an upright piano to the porch, and members of an African American church choir assembled on the steps to sing "Amazing Grace." As their powerful voices rose over the potato fields, I knew there was no way I was going to follow "Amazing

Grace" with "Are You from Dixie." I went to the bar, ordered a fresh Bloody Mary, and faded into the potato fields. John and Jenny were speech and drama majors. They'd do just fine without me.

I lingered in the potatoes for upward of an hour. When I returned Dean told me that Willie had introduced our friends as his "latest discovery" and that they'd sung "Are You from Dixie" *a cappella*.

Davis came looking for me, indignantly picked me up like a sack of potatoes, and carried me around on his shoulder in case anyone wanted to see what an arrant coward looked like.

Pulling out all the stops Willie wangled invitations for us to attend Budd Shulberg's wedding reception the following day. Fifteen minutes after we arrived at the Montauk Yacht Club I was standing at the bar when I noticed a beautiful woman kick off her shoes and wade in the surf with Irwin Shaw. I wasn't jealous of Irwin, just admiring the woman's easy smile, dark hair blowing in her face, the athletic grace with which she skipped over the low waves. As the couple came closer the lovely woman passed through the frame of my vision.

My god, I thought, that's my wife!

The next night we had dinner at the home of Grace Corlitz and her husband, the North Carolina artist Warren Brandt. Irwin Shaw met us at the door, drew Dean into the dining room, and indicated two chairs that he'd propped on the table. She was to sit next to him. Dean was like a cat with cream on its whiskers. Not as pretty as she'd looked skipping waves with Irwin.

At dinner she not only sat beside Irwin but held hands with him under the table. Granted he was in his seventies but he had a legendary reputation as a ladies' man. She made a feeble attempt to eat with her left hand.

Seated to her left was author Joseph Heller, who, when he saw she wasn't eating, asked if he could have her food. He explained that he'd played handball that day and was starving. She acted as if Joseph Heller ate off her plate every day. This was a Dean I'd never seen before. Meanwhile, my dinner partners, Craig Claiborne and John Knowles, pretended to compete for my attention. Dean and I were both getting hit on, but only one of us was enjoying it. "There's a Catch 22 for you," I thought as Heller gobbled her untouched food.

After dinner Willie organized a "nightcap" session at the Triple Crown. Those over seventy said goodnight and retired for the evening. I reclaimed my wife and stayed at her side throughout the drinks and dancing that followed.

Two nightcaps later I was hoping to make it to the motel without being arrested. Gloria and her guests began leaving. Morris blocked the entrance and dramatically clung to the door frame.

"Don't leave me, don't leave me!" he begged, falling to his knees and clutching at people's legs as they left. Dean and I glanced at each other. Willie's Hampton friends took his silly behavior for granted and avoided him in a practiced way. Whereas Oxford treated Willie like a saint, Bridgehampton refused to put up with his antics.

Introducing us to his Hampton circle had been a way of paying us back. But perhaps Willie also wanted to see how his Long Island friends would react to us and conversely how we would behave in such lofty company. Or maybe Willie's "last stand" in the barroom door meant that he indeed was having second thoughts about moving back to Mississippi.

"Home, as the old words say, is where the heart is," he wrote in *Terrains of the Heart and Other Essays on Home*. "But where, then, is the heart?"

III. Rivals in Residence

- 16 -

Barry

He looked like a young Marlon Brando, his black hair bound by a red bandana, military dog tags dangling from a chain around his neck, black T-shirt with the sleeves cut off, jeans with holes at the knees. He played with a bowie knife, sticking it into the floor over and over. Our host that evening was Ole Miss professor Louis Dollarhide, who'd been Barry Hannah's mentor at Mississippi College. He introduced Dean and me, saying that Hannah had been his favorite student "long ago and far away." As soon as Dollarhide left to fix drinks Hannah turned to me, knife in hand.

"I could overpower you and take your woman," he said.

"You'll have to fight both of us," Dean replied. I was charmed by her quick comeback and so was Hannah. She instinctively understood that he was flirting with her. Encouraged by Dean's reparteé Hannah stopped playing with his knife and began telling us about a fighter pilot shot down in Vietnam. I assumed he was referring to a friend in the air force. "Got careless and was shot down by a ground-to-air missile, parachuted into the jungle, evaded the Viet Cong for two weeks, and walked out unscathed." Grinning boyishly, he waited to be congratulated. I was pretty sure Hannah hadn't flown Phantom jets in Vietnam. Was he trying out a fictional character on us? Just then Dollarhide returned with the drinks.

"Barry, please take it easy on the vodka," he murmured.

"Did you see the ski boat?" said Hannah.

"Couldn't miss it," said Dean referring to the motorboat and trailer parked in Dollarhide's lawn.

"I pulled off the highway east of Oxford to take a leak," Hannah explained. "In the woods was a sixteen-foot fiberglass ski boat. Some generous SOB left it for me," he added as if stunned by his good fortune. He'd driven into Oxford, purchased a trailer hitch, and returned before another SOB could steal his boat. "Good deal, huh?"

"Do y'all know anyone who will come and take that boat away?" Dollarhide lamented.

Barry Hannah was on the run. He'd been fired by the University of Alabama for bringing a revolver to class. It was unloaded but the students didn't know that. Hearing that Ole Miss was planning to hire Morris, Hannah had come job hunting at Ole Miss.

Ordinary conversation bored Hannah. Like a ninja warrior attacking the dullness of human existence he interrupted one of us in mid-sentence. "Read living writers! No disrespect to your relative, Dean." He drained the glass of vodka and went to the window to check on his abandoned boat. This meant that he was ready to go.

Willie was waiting in his driveway at 16 Faculty Row. He'd never met Barry but claimed to be a fan of his work. Earlier, when I'd mentioned *Airships*, Barry's prize-winning short story collection, Willie didn't seem to recognize the title. I recommended Hannah's autobiographical novel, *Geronimo Rex*. On the way to the Sizzler Restaurant the authors exchanged the usual obligatory compliments; then Hannah asked Willie, just making conversation, "How tough are the cops in Oxford. They never let us have any fun, do they!" He paused. "So, are you *the* writer-in-residence?"

"I guess so," Willie said.

Things were getting off to a shaky start.

At the Sizzler, Hannah proceeded to get roaring drunk, at one point mixing wine with bourbon.

"Barry, did you mean to mix wine and whiskey?" asked Willie.

Hannah frowned. "Didn't you ever hear of a Mississippi Manhattan?"

Morris adored writers drunk or sober. He didn't mind when a novelist tried out a new character in casual conversation, if that's what Hannah was up to. Dean, however, looked worried. While she loved writers, she drew the line at behaving in a disorderly or boorish fashion.

On the way back to town I drove. Willie sat in the front passenger seat, and Dean in the rear seat with the Phantom pilot. Willie resumed a football discussion he'd begun at dinner.

"Ole Miss athletics have leveled the playing field between the races," he observed. "There's hope for Mississippi yet, don't you agree?" He took a reflective sip of bolla bardolino, adding before I could reply, "And at the same time continuity with the past!"

Dean was half-listening to this familiar incantation when she felt a hand on her left breast. She crossed her arms, not shocked, not exactly, given Hannah's state of inebriation. She figured she could brush him off, except—what had he said? *I could overpower you and take your woman*. He tried to kiss her. She twisted and turned, fought in silence. If she made a scene Willie would tell everyone, and that would be the end of Hannah's hopes of teaching at Ole Miss. Hannah, as she well knew, was at a crossroads. What he needed wasn't a feel but a hand up. And Oxford's literary den mother wasn't about to dash his chances. Given the headlight glare in my rearview mirror I could not see what was happening in the rear seat.

". . . He said the rebel flags aren't meant to embarrass blacks," Willie optimistically quoted an African American running back. "He's not disturbed by the sight of Confederate battle flags on the Ole Miss campus. To him they are just an expression of school spirit. That's a progress of sorts, wouldn't you say?"

"Uncle Tom in a football helmet!" grunted Hannah, the multitasker.

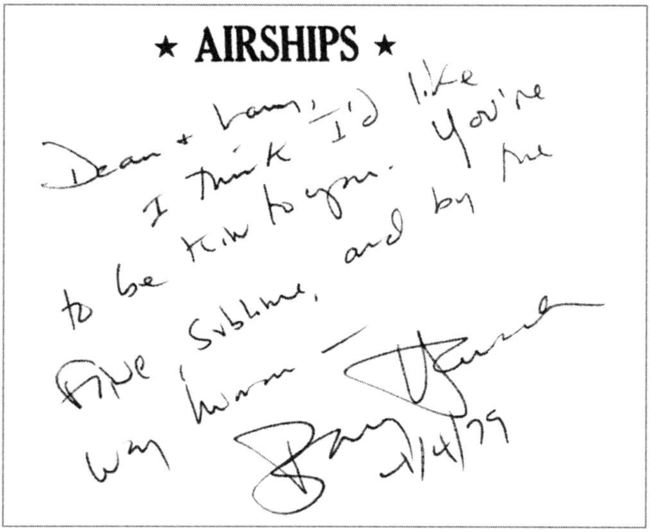

"No, Barry, Ole Miss will come around," said Willie without glancing over his shoulder. "I know they will! Penitence is usually followed by vindication, then amity, then hope. What did Pappy say, Deanie? Hope ain't all we need, it's all we've got!"

No reply came from the rear seat, "Deanie" being preoccupied. She was doubtless thinking that when she told Hannah he would have to fight both of us she didn't expect him to take her seriously. Arm-strength waning, she remembered the "Chi Omega Clamp," a self-defense tactic that her sorority sisters taught incoming freshmen. With her right hand she pinned Barry's left arm around her neck, then gripped his right wrist with her left hand. Locked together in a Mississippi version of American Gothic they panted from their exertions. Here was a breed of woman Hannah had never met or imagined—one who resisted without judging or resenting. The author of *Geronimo Rex* would soon place her on a pedestal, saying to anyone who would listen, "That scrappy Faulkner woman is like a Sioux squaw. She'll stake herself next to her dead husband and fight to the death."

To Dean's surprise Hannah laid his head on her shoulder and feigned sleep, his breathing as deep and unhurried as a child's. On long car trips Dean's children had dozed on her shoulder in much the same way. Amused at this boyish solution she played along.

Meanwhile, Willie turned to the really important question of the day: "But . . . can Ole Miss win the SEC?"

The white Oldsmobile continued on its return to Oxford. I was the driver charged with getting us back safely, Willie the conductor punching tickets and musing on football and civil rights, Barry, enfant terrible, dozing on the shoulder of literature, and Dean chained to Hannah's pedestal. If she spilled the beans, Ole Miss students would be denied the benefit of his teaching; and Willie would miss the pleasure of sparring with him. On a soft spring night four grown children roamed the Mississippi byroads, and only one of us knew the way home.

That same spring, Northwest Mississippi Community College invited Hannah to speak at Sycamore Fair, the annual arts festival. The school's honorarium was a modest $300 but Hannah accepted. He then phoned us asking if it would "be a problem" for us to introduce him to the Ole Miss English department faculty. We agreed, and Dean began organizing a buffet dinner in his honor. This, after all, was why she'd saved Hannah from his self-destructive tendencies.

Student attendance was mandatory at Hannah's lecture. Most of the students filing into the NWCC auditorium had never heard of him. It mattered not that *Airships* had won a prestigious literary award or that Hannah was a bold new voice in American letters or that *Esquire* had published three dozen of his short stories. Resigned to attending the program they took their seats. It was a tough sell but Hannah wouldn't have had it any other way. He went to the podium and asked, "What do y'all do for fun?"

Dead silence. *Who was this guy? Did he expect them to give out personal information?* Hannah pointed at a student in the front row who hesitantly answered.

"Not a whole lot . . . *sir*." This got a laugh.

"Ain't nothing *to* do!" a female student volunteered, receiving an even louder laugh.

"When Kroger's closes at ten," said another student, "we park in the parking lot and sit in our cars and see who comes by." Hannah was taking notes by then.

"*No, sir, officer, we ain't drinking no beer,*" cracked a jokester. The students roared. Smelling story Hannah kept them talking. And when they ran out of things to say, he paraphrased his notes, composing a narrative.

> *Life begins at Kroger's. Ease into the parking lot. Turn up the radio to let your pals know you're there. The cops drive by real slow. They never let you have any fun. "No sir, officer dear, we ain't drinking no suds." After the cops leave, we lock and load. Who's coming? Who's going? Who's gone? Sometimes days and nights get glued together. All you can do is hope things will get better, hope life is gonna be okay. Then a couple in a pickup start making out, and everybody honks their horns, and it's all right, man. It's all right.*

The students rose as one, whistled through their fingers, beat on the backs of seats. A Mississippi god of words had come down from Blue Mountain or wherever such gods lived to tell their story. *Theirs!* Barry Hannah got them. He spoke their language. This wasn't all there was to their lives, not by a long shot, but Saturday night at Kroger's wasn't a bad place to start.

Beaming like Baby Jesus, Hannah asked if there were any questions. The students clammed up, though shy and appreciative. He had defined them. Nothing more need be said. Hannah nodded in approval.

"Yeah," he said.

The festival coordinator raised her hand asking if Hannah used a similar method in his creative writing classes. Barry winked at Dean.

"Naw, I just tell 'em to read Faulkner," he grinned.

That evening Dean prepared dinner for the English department faculty, and I went to get wine. Barry had checked into the Holiday Inn. Earlier he'd remarked that he was "big on Oxford," which for him was high praise and, to us, an indication he wanted to teach at Ole Miss. The professors and their wives began arriving at seven. We served drinks and dinner. Still no Barry! I phoned the Holiday Inn bar asking if there was a guy in a motorcycle jacket talking about Vietnam. Clyde Goolsby, Oxford's venerable bartender, said, "Yeah, would you come get him?"

I asked Jack Crocker, our colleague at NWCC, to entertain the guests with his guitar. By the time I returned with Hannah in tow, half of the English faculty members were gone. I was making introductions when, ignoring acting department chairman Evan Harrington's outstretched hand, Hannah grabbed Crocker's guitar and began doing a Jimi Hendrix imitation.

The following day, Harrington phoned to report that the response was divided. The faculty wondered if they could take a chance on Hannah.

"Are you kidding?" I said. "Even if Hannah lasts only a year what other southern university can match the Willie and Barry show?"

- 17 -

Hannah Steals Faulkner's *Big Woods*

BEFORE RETURNING TO TUSCALOOSA HANNAH DROPPED BY to say goodbye. He asked if he could borrow Dean's personal copy of Faulkner's *Big Woods: The Hunting Stories*, which was inscribed "To my girl Dean, Love, Pappy." Between Hendrix impersonations Hannah must have browsed our bookshelves. He wanted to be able "just to hold it for a while." To my horror Dean let him walk out of the house with it. He promptly left town and took the book back to Tuscaloosa. Like the abandoned motorboat it was a found object.

She wrote Hannah asking that he return the book. Two months passed without a reply. On the way to visit my family in Alabama I stopped at Hannah's house in Tuscaloosa. As it happened he was being interviewed for *Playboy*. I apologized for interrupting. "I'll just pick up Dean's book," I said, "and leave you guys to it." Hannah changed the subject. Could I help the *Playboy* writer? He'd also interviewed Coach Bear Bryant but couldn't decipher what was being said on the tape. Hannah asked me to help them interpret Bryant's bear-like drawl. Anything to put off the inevitable.

I seized on the coincidence that *Big Woods* was about a bear hunt. Hannah notched an arrow in a crossbow, cocked it, went to the front door, and shot toward a house across the street. The arrow slammed into a neighbor's door. Hannah pointed at the result. "Bulls-eye," he said.

Faulkner's niece had sent her dead husband to retrieve a trophy meant for a warrior. Didn't she know Hannah would give his life for her? No Phantom pilot would seek the return of a book entrusted to an author who'd won the American Academy's highest award and was doing his damnedest to pull the fucking rabbit out of the fucking hat every day no matter the sacrifice. An arrow from his crossbow to the late husband's gut would be an honor to say the least.

Finally seeing that I wasn't intimidated and would not leave without my wife's book, he went to a shelf, extracted *Big Woods*, and reluctantly handed it over.

- 18 -

Rivals in Residence

THE ENGLISH DEPARTMENT INVITED HANNAH TO JOIN THE faculty. Soon he became a familiar sight riding to class on his Harley in a sleeveless T-shirt and sporting a Blue Angels tattoo. His classes were the stuff of legend. Then weeks into the semester Hannah began complaining about his rival-in-residence. "Willie is an essayist, not a fiction writer. Why not call him 'Journalist in Residence' or something like that?"

Willie did not respond publicly but in private observed that the university could call him "any damned thing they like—sportswriter in residence or gag writer in residence."

After Hannah's first semester things settled down. For a while it appeared that the writers had reached an accommodation. When *Ray*, Hannah's latest novel, was published Willie invited him to celebrate at the Gumbo Company, a new bar on the square (later to become Syd and Harry's). Hannah sipped a martini, ate the olive, and said, "Willie, I write the truth and you write public relations."

"*I felt like slugging the guy!*" Morris told us. "There I was, doing my best to be nice and he comes out swinging with his . . . his . . . relentless one-up-man-ship." Hannah's problem as far as we could see was that to the press Willie had become the university's unofficial spokesperson. If a campus incident occurred it was Morris that the *New York Times* or *Newsweek* contacted, not Hannah, who with his penchant for exaggeration was not to be taken seriously.

It was as if Hannah's characters were speaking for him. His own super-creativity had taken him hostage.

For the most part Morris refused to recognize that a rivalry existed. As a former editor his first instinct was to support writers, not compete with them. Experience had taught him that writers, in particular fiction writers, were high maintenance. For example, his pal Norman Mailer, trapped by fetishes and bored with ordinary life, attacked those closest to him. To Morris such emotional outbursts were a hazard of the trade. All that mattered was a writer's life on paper, what he or she left on the printed page.

After the "public relations" remark Morris suppressed his resentment, paid the bar tab, and escorted Hannah to Square Books. He even bought the first copy of *Ray* and asked Hannah to inscribe it. One would like to believe Barry was touched by Willie's magnanimity.

Hannah became a regular at Square Books, which was soon to be named the "Best Independent Bookstore in the U.S." At the coffee counter upstairs he chain-smoked, drank cinnamon coffee, and scribbled story ideas about drifters, dope dealers, whores, thieves, killers, and ordinary tradesmen with violent tendencies. "My work is about pain," he said.

One summer night when I was out of town Hannah pulled up at 510 South Lamar in a convertible. "Get your daughters ready," he told Dean (meaning Diane, twenty-two, and Paige, twenty). "I'm taking y'all to the Jimmy Buffett concert on Mud Island."

Diane's fiancé, Michael Cawley, was there, and Dean agreed to go if Hannah let Michael drive. At 6'4" a graduate student in psychology and part-time bartender, Cawley was the ideal designated driver/peacemaker. Hannah sat in the rear seat between Paige and Dean. He poured margaritas into Dixie cups while Diane lit cigarettes with the car's lighter and passed them back. The radio was playing music Dean did not recognize.

"Heavy metal," Michael murmured diplomatically.

"What planet have you been on, Mama?" Paige asked.

At Mud Island having switched to daiquiris they danced in the aisle, shouted the lyrics to "Margaritaville," and made Jimmy Buffett sing until his voice gave out. After the concert Hannah talked his way backstage while Paige and Diane collected the stories of Buffett-groupies whose mothers, Paige reported, wore tie-dyed T-shirts identical to those of their daughters. "Before Buffett came along they were Elvis freaks!" added Paige. When Dean remarked that she'd attended an Elvis concert in Tupelo in 1956, Paige gave her a playful shove. "The point is, Mama, you got over it!"

Emerging from the dressing room Hannah grinned as the groupies peppered him with questions about Buffett. When it was clear he wasn't in the band, they lost interest. "Aren't there any *readers* here?" he lamented. Dean was miffed that Hannah hadn't taken her to meet Jimmy. "Why didn't you come get us?" she said.

Hannah looked stricken. "I thought you preferred fiction writers."

Returning to Mississippi the group turned off I-55 at the Sardis exit where they were stopped by local police. When an officer shined a flashlight into the car, Hannah handed Dean his Dixie cup. Spotting a tequila bottle the officer ordered Michael to follow him to the station. Dean's designated driver-in-law had limited himself to a couple of beers, but just in case, on the way to the station, Hannah fed him doughnuts, saying, "Sugar burns alcohol, baby." Dean was about to telephone for help when Cawley emerged from the station. He'd passed the breathalyzer test.

As they drove away from the station, Hannah yelled into the Sardis night, "*What the hell does it take to get arrested in the state of Mississippi!*"

- 19 -

The Feud

Born on April 23, Shakespeare's birthday, Barry Hannah blew into the world fully formed. His debut novel *Geronimo Rex*, begun at the University of Arkansas when he was a graduate student, was nominated for a National Book Award. His short story collection, *Airships*, won the Award in Literature from the American Academy and Institute of Arts and Letters. The novelist Tom McGuane once told me, "Barry Hannah writes like an angel." A dark angel, that is, who lived through his characters, followed them into real life and egged them on. Any well-conceived character, Hannah liked to say, could write his own story.

As I Lay Dying, which Faulkner wrote in a reported six weeks on the back of a wheelbarrow, was Hannah's favorite novel. The idea of Faulkner working the night shift as a fire stoker at the Ole Miss power plant appealed to Barry's burning sense of purpose. And the Bundrens' biblical journey with a stinking coffin, the wagon submerging in a flooded river, the coffin washing downstream, was the story of Mississippi's (and Faulkner's) struggle for recognition.

"That's a novel I wish I'd written," Hannah told me.

Hannah's non sequiturs and off-the-wall progressions reminded me of comedian Jonathan Winters. When I asked if this was intentional, Hannah gave me a startled, appreciative glance. His publisher at Grove/Atlantic, Morgan Entrekin, summed up *Geronimo Rex* as "gonzo southern fiction that opened you to a whole new way of writing."

"Hannah is an original," wrote Ivan Gold, "or if names are to be dropped, Carson McCullers rewritten by Groucho Marx."

When Hannah was a graduate student at the University of Arkansas in 1965, two of his professors, James Whitehead and Bill Harrison, established a creative writing program. Hannah submitted a sample chapter from *Geronimo Rex*. Whitehead brought Harrison the manuscript.

"We've got our anchor," he told Harrison.

Hannah's career took off with the publication of a short story called "Mother Rooney Unscrolls the Hurt." In *Wayback* magazine, Hannah observed:

> And then I wrote my first truly good story, "Mother Rooney Unscrolls the Hurt," which was a piece of my then-forthcoming book, Geronimo Rex. I was about 23. It really lit up for me, I thought. I don't really care what folks think of it now, but "Mother Rooney" was a springboard to the rest of my creative life.

All writers begin as book fiends, eggheads, and smart-alecks. As fuel for fiction they nurture neuroses and hang onto slights endured in junior high.

"Hannah scared the hell out of me," said Harrison. "He carried a pistol in his back pocket. You never knew when he'd go off the deep end."

I was with Hannah when a Dutch radio host interviewed him at Oxford's Gin Company. When Hannah compared reading a well-known American writer's work to playing pinball—"*It's fun while it lasts but in the end you walk away with nothing!*"—I interrupted and changed the subject. Later Hannah marveled, "You had my back, buddy!"

We were fishing buddies, football fans, and fellow scribes. Always, the last week in August, Hannah phoned me saying, "Time for a football fix." He couldn't wait for SEC football season to begin. For twenty years we attended an Oxford High game together in late August.

After six publishers turned down *The Tennis Handsome*, Hannah offered the novel to Yoknapatawpha Press. Dean and I were delighted. By then we'd published three books by Willie Morris (*Good Old Boy, Terrains of the Heart, North Toward Home*) and the prospect of adding Hannah to the Yok Press stable was a dream come true. We shook hands on the deal, and Hannah gave me the manuscript saying, "See if you can fix it, okay?"

One doesn't edit Hannah any more than Saxe Commins dared correct Faulkner's punctuation. Writing for his severest critic—himself—Hannah began every novel with a "decent" sentence. "And then I try to write another sentence just as strong, and another one. And when the sentences stop coming I know the story is finished."

He'd based *The Tennis Handsome* on a magazine assignment about a professional tennis player. After attending several tournaments Hannah got bored with reality and created "Baby Levaster," the manager of tennis pro "French Edward," who requires a jolt of lightning to improve his playing. Fiction to Hannah, I think, was a kind of therapy, highly superior to life.

It was clear why publishers had rejected *The Tennis Handsome*. While it contained the usual brilliant wordplay, it lacked cohesion. There were dead ends, acrobatic digressions, bats out of hell flying in circles. My job was to restore narrative flow while retaining Hannah's tone and voice. The story was there but in the wrong places. Without altering the language I shifted passages, in some cases whole chapters. It took three weeks to edit and retype the manuscript. (No computers back then.)

I asked Hannah to review the edited manuscript. Prepared to be disappointed, he sat down in our basement office across from Neilson's Department Store. While he speed-read the manuscript I busied myself with nonessential duties. I heard him muttering, "Yeah, yeah . . . *yeah*!" Then he gathered up the manuscript and

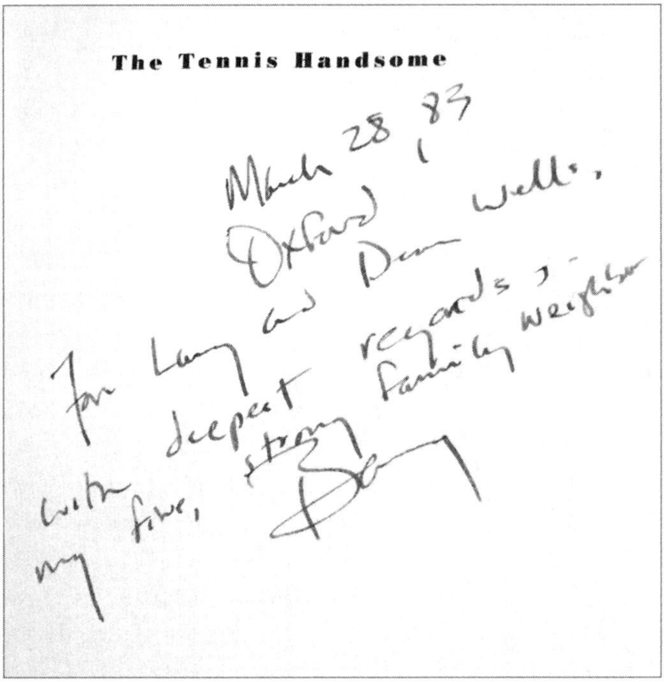

said, "I'll take this with me. See you later." And he was gone. A month later I heard that Knopf had bought *The Tennis Handsome*. When the book came out, Ivan Gold exulted: "There is endless instruction and delight in watching [Hannah] refine his idiosyncratic vision, chipping away at the block of marble, fashioning a Yoknapatawpha County of the mind."

Barry and I never spoke of his having reneged on our agreement. He obliquely apologized by co-dedicating *The Tennis Handsome* to me and his motorcycle buddy, Larry DeBord, who'd kept Barry occupied while I was editing the manuscript.

If life wasn't entertaining, Barry made it up. The contretemps with Willie was mostly Barry's doing. Either he envied the affection Oxford showered on his rival or he sought controversy for its own sake. Hannah and Edgar Allen Poe would have been best pals up until the moment they drew pistols.

Morris liked Hannah but instinct made him hold back. Having worked closely with writers at *Harper's* he respected Hannah's achievements; but "gonzo southern fiction" wasn't his thing. Where they were of one mind was an obsession with their literary standing. In Mississippi it's all about who takes the baton from Faulkner.

Willie wanted to be loved. Hannah wanted to be feared. Where Morris was a literary ambassador, Hannah peddled literary methamphetamine. Seeking local color in his stories he "outed" several professors who practiced alternate lifestyles.

Willie was a son of the Delta to whom whiskey was the oil of conversation. He composed controlled and balanced essays. He was the voice of the southern intelligentsia. His daily schedule was to write from two until eight p.m. Then he'd hit the bars and, after last call, take students, alumni, and the occasional traveling salesman home with him. Everyone had a story, and Morris took mental notes. He never forgot anything. Weeks or months later funny, quirky stories collected at four in the morning poured out of him. Locals loved reading about themselves. Willie could be trusted to chronicle their "good side." If Faulkner was dark as night and Hannah a shadow-boxer, Morris was a lost soul searching for home.

A couple of months after the "you write public relations" remark, Morris decided it was time to shake hands and make up. The editor in him never gave up on writers no matter how crazy—though he confided that he'd given up trying to *read* Hannah, whom he lumped in with "the generation of verbal gymnasts who juggle words until the whole story is up in the air." Willie asked me to drive him to Hannah's rental house west of town. I wasn't sure this was a good idea but did as he asked.

From Hannah's driveway we could hear Jimi Hendrix at full volume within the house. I knocked on the door. Getting no response Morris and I let ourselves in. The combined living room and dining room had no furniture except a trap drum set and a stereo with oversized speakers. Hannah was beating out a wild rhythm on the drums, eyes closed, cigarette dangling from his lips. He didn't acknowledge our presence. Not even a simple nod. When the record ended he set the drumsticks aside and sauntered toward us. Morris prepared himself to bury the hatchet.

"*Hot damn, a deer!*" Hannah shouted. Whipping a pistol from behind his back he fired twice through a screened door. Deafened, cordite filling my nostrils, I turned to look in Morris's direction. He was running out the door.

To Barry, shooting Willie in effigy, just as he'd "shot me" with his crossbow, must have seemed a bold and fabulous prank. I could only imagine how he rationalized it: *Hey, it was only a ritual shooting, for Christ's sake. If Willie didn't get it, he fundamentally lacked a sense of humor. If a writer wants to be worthy of his gun-packing characters he has to justify them by his actions.*

After that day Morris was never alone with Hannah. Now and then they ran into each other in public. Writers have problems with life. Prose is easily fixed.

- 20 -

The Hoka Theatre

PRINCESS HOKA, DAUGHTER OF CHIEF PONTOTOC, LEADER OF the Chickasaws, was a little-known historical figure until Ron Shapiro, a native of St. Louis, moved to Oxford in 1975 and named his second-run movie theater after her.

If Willie Morris brought literary glamour to town and campus, Shapiro made movie-going not just fun but compulsory. Suddenly great films were available in Oxford at second-run prices. "Ronzo's" encyclopedic knowledge of film history and his taste in modern films turned Oxford into a movie-going town. Students flocked to the Hoka, housed in what had been an empty cotton warehouse next to the Gin Company, for cinnamon-flavored coffee, a turkey club sandwich called "Love-at-First-Bite," and the classic Hoka cheesecake. You could order Love-at-First-Bite, buy tickets to the movie, and have your meal served inside the theater. We held Dean's fiftieth birthday bash at the Hoka.

Shapiro's sidekick, ticket-taker, and projector operator, the inimitable Barton Segal, had a style all his own. Frat boys in the audience would heckle Barton while he was changing reels just to provoke him into shouting, "Fuck you!"

This rustic second-run theater allowed us to catch up on films such as *Jaws, Blazing Saddles, Raiders of the Lost Ark, Aliens, Back to the Future, Full Metal Jacket.* But the Hoka was much more than a second-run movie theater/coffee shop. To paraphrase Faulkner, it was a cosmos of Ronzo's own. As a graduate student, my son

Lawrence waited tables at the Hoka. My stepson Jon worked the counter and watched second-run movies on his break. Jim Dees, later to become the long-standing emcee of the *Thacker Mountain Radio Show*, tried out his monologues at the Hoka. Buck, Jamo, Semmes, and Ollie were cultural ambassadors posing as cooks and waiters.

Morris loved the Hoka not for its movies but the fact that Shapiro kept it open after the bars closed. After midnight Willie usually could be found sitting on a stool at the Hoka counter sipping coffee laced with bourbon. As a bachelor on Long Island in the 1970s Morris cultivated a cadre of hostesses willing to put on dinner parties. In Oxford he counted on the Willie-Altar-Guild and Ron Shapiro to help entertain his guests.

When Alex Haley was invited to speak at the University of Mississippi, Willie as senior writer-in-residence asked Ronzo to put on a dinner in Haley's honor. Shapiro, who enjoyed hosting special events such as this, generously obliged. But to defray his expenses he sold $5 tickets (the standard price of a movie at the Hoka) and billed the event as "An Evening with Alex Haley." Willie was to introduce Haley, and their repartee would theoretically entertain the audience while Ronzo and guest chef Jane Rule Burdine cooked pork chops, cabbage, blackeyed peas, and cornbread. Distressed at this deviation from usual programming Barton Segal, ticket booth clerk, projector operator, and film savant, apologized to incoming patrons as he sold tickets.

Willie's dinner guests included Masaru Inoue, a Faulkner scholar from Ferris University in Yokohama; Alex Haley and his publicist; Dean and me; and four African American football players selected at random "to make Haley feel at home." Willie admitted that he had asked Coach Billy Brewer to "send over some black players to meet Haley."

Due to the bright stage lights it was not easy for us "cast members" to see the audience. Eventually I spotted Barry Hannah among the paying customers looking like a grim Alfred E. Newman. The last time Willie had seen Hannah he'd been looking down the barrel of a Ruger magnum pistol. No wonder he forgot to include Barry on the guest list.

As Willie introduced Masaru Inoue to Haley, Hannah was incredulous. Professor Inoue bowed to Haley and made a short speech praising *Roots* and Haley's worldwide influence. It was a Mississippi happening given an enrapt audience surrounding an angry Hannah and the football players who dwarfed their fellow diners and were respectful even though their coach hadn't explained why they had been dispatched to the Hoka to eat dinner on a stage with people they didn't know.

"At the welcoming dinner for Alex Haley on December 3, 1986," Inoue recalled, "I gave an address in Japanese, which confused Mr. Haley. He could only respond with a chuckle. Willie offered an English translation saying, 'Listen, Alex, I will translate Masaru's words into English, word for word.' Willie gave Haley the translation and urged me to give him a copy also of the Japanese version, which I did." This is the text of Professor Inoue's introduction:

> Ten years ago when I read *Roots*, it reminded me that individual human beings are like small islands in the ocean. They seem to be isolated and separated from the continent, but they are linked to the continent by the bottom of the ocean. Even though mankind seems to be separated, independent and isolated he is part of the whole. In *Roots* Alex Haley dug a tunnel between the continent and the islands.

At the back of the auditorium, resplendent in chef's apron, Ronzo nodded with pleasure. The famous diners' program seemed to be going well. Professor Inoue was great theater worth the price of admission, as were the stunned and irate mutterings of Hannah. *What was this travesty to which he hadn't been given a courtesy invite? A Japanese twilight zone which even the late, great Rod Serling couldn't have made up?* In the projection box near the rafters Barton Segal shook his head in disgust. Once again his boss had cooked up more than pork chops and cabbage. Haley, guest of honor, seemed mercifully unaware that a dozen or so Hoka regulars had paid to watch him dine. Inoue extolled the stage lights which seemed to create rings around the atoll of the stage. Ronzo's paying customers represented coral reefs attached to Morris and Haley, twin islands of genius, while we diners were Inoue's Greek chorus.

"What is this shit?" shouted Hannah, the exile. "Get this fucking show on the road!"

I could see it dawning on Willie that he'd neglected to invite Hannah. Embarrassed he stood and called Hannah to the stage. But the authors of *Geronimo Rex* and *Roots* had no such island linking their continents.

"How are you, Alex?" asked Hannah.

"Nice to meet you, Barry," Haley replied.

Satisfied at having finally been acknowledged Hannah delivered his customary benediction—"*Yeah!*"—and left the building. I wondered if Ronzo's customers recognized that this convergence of the twain was worth roughly ten times the price of admission.

Knowing a comedy of errors when he saw one, Haley turned to the football players.

"You're a Hausa!" he told the athlete seated on his right. The players were shocked. Was the gentleman talking about them? Haley went on identifying each football player's African American genetic group by facial features. Turning to the two players to his left, he continued, "You're Yoruga, and you're probably, no, definitely, Kalenjin." Suppressing their irritation, the athletes glanced at each other as if to say *What the hell! We are Americans.*

Dinner was two hours late. Ronzo explained that the cooks "might have smoked some weed." Willie didn't mind. With Jack Daniel's and Viceroys he was set until the millennium. At ten o'clock pork chops, cabbage, blackeyed peas, and cornbread appeared. We'd been waiting three hours. With the exception of Hannah, the amazingly loyal audience had stuck it out.

"Is this enough food for you?" I asked the massive linebacker opposite to me.

"I ate before I came," he whispered.

- 21 -

Jimmy Buffett

JIMMY BUFFETT WAS PERFORMING IN MEMPHIS WHEN SEMMES Luckett, of Clarksdale, Mississippi, told him about us. Luckett had been Hunter Thompson's social secretary when Jimmy hired him as road social manager. At Ole Miss in the 1960s and 1970s Luckett was legendary for remaining an undergraduate for thirteen years.

We happened to be giving a Faulkner Conference cocktail party when Luckett brought Jimmy to the house. We took them to a picnic at Rowan Oak. Buffett tried in vain to remain anonymous, but the Faulkner scholars surrounded him seeking autographs. One would have thought we'd brought William Faulkner to his own faux party.

Back at the house, as guests socialized with Willie Morris and Barry Hannah, Buffett grazed on asparagus salad and drank a Black Velvet, a mixture of Guinness and champagne, which according to Dean was "Pappy's sailing drink."

A few minutes later I overheard Jimmy singing "Margaritaville" *a capella* in the kitchen. He was serenading Dean's daughters, Paige, then eighteen, and Diane, twenty. I gave Jimmy my Sears Silvertone guitar, apologizing for the nylon strings, and grabbed my string bass. I was delirious at the chance to back up Buffett. Within minutes the kitchen was packed with listeners. Through the window I noticed college students assembling in the yard. The word was out that Jimmy Buffett was at 510 South Lamar.

Hannah grew restless and took off, causing someone to observe, "Barry's jealous of Buffett!" Whereas Morris, seated at the table, his back to the wall as usual, said, "The students didn't come to see Jimmy Buffett. They came to see Semmes Luckett."

Before Buffett returned to Memphis, Dean told him the story of the Absalom table.

Ten years later when Jimmy was playing another concert at Mud Island, he gave us a copy of his stage play entitled, *An Evening in Margaritaville*, a two-act play by Jimmy Buffett and Bob Dubal based on an original short story by Jimmy Buffett. This play would later become the basis for the Broadway production *Escape to Margaritaville*. Sitting at the Absalom table Buffett inscribed the script to us.

But the most important thing Buffett did was introduce us to his mother, Loraine Peets Buffett. Jimmy was playing a concert in New Orleans the same weekend we were planning to attend the Mississippi Library Conference on the Gulf Coast. Jimmy promised us passes to the concert.

Before we left for the coast Dean came down with the twenty-four-hour flu. On the way to New Orleans she asked me to stop at a liquor store for medicinal alcohol. Between Jackson and New Orleans she downed two and a half screwdrivers. By the time we reached the Sanger Theatre her flu was history.

As Buffett's band tuned up before the concert, the Parrotheads in the audience warmed up by smoking pot. Noticing backstage passes plastered to our shirts, several offered Dean and me a hit.

"Do you know Jimmy?" one of the fans asked. "Is he a good guy?"

We danced in the aisle during the show and afterward went backstage to what can only be described as a holding room for groupies. After thirty minutes Jimmy, accompanied by bodyguards and determined not to make eye contact with the groupies, scurried through the room.

"*Jimmy Buffett!*" Dean yelled. Bent over he froze and pointed at his bodyguard.

"Deanie," Jimmy said without looking at her, "*he* will bring you to *me*." Then he dived into the backseat of a waiting limo. The bodyguard came back and plastered K-Paul passes on our shirts.

We made our way to K-Paul's Restaurant through an alcoholic fog and were soon in the delightful company of the wise and witty Peets Buffett, a fun-loving spirit who taught Dean the secret of living in a famous relative's shadow.

"You can't change who you are," she told Dean, "so relax and enjoy the ride."

It's amazing how a philosophy this simple could be so transforming. These were words Dean had been waiting to hear. Peets understood her struggle for identity in a way no one else had. With this casual but heartfelt bit of practical advice, she changed Dean's life, and for over two decades until Peets's death in 2003 they were soul sisters.

- 22 -

Oxford's Literary Renaissance

When *The Sound and the Fury* was published William Faulkner was not merely a one-man show in Oxford but a firestorm scorching the planet. After he died the town was at a loss. Who would take his place? How could the town uphold the literary legacy Faulkner had left behind? The first step was for someone to open a bookstore where Faulkner's books could be sold.

Enter, with the blessings of the gods, Square Books.

In 1977 Richard and Lisa Howorth opened Square Books on the east side of the square in a second-floor walkup. The week before they opened, Richard had some empty shelf space to fill temporarily. I brought him two boxes of John Faulkner's books, *Dollar Cotton* and *My Brother, Bill*, which Yoknapatawpha Press had reprinted. Richard helped me carry the boxes upstairs. From that day on, Oxford's town square was filled with the adventure and possibility that only books can bring.

An independent bookstore is a place where kindred spirits gather to discuss books and exchange ideas. Square Books soon evolved into a birthplace of writers. John Grisham's first major book signing for *The Firm* occurred here. The line of fans stretched outside the store and around the square. Jesmyn Ward, Jonathan Miles, Donna Tartt, Steve Yarborough, Ace Atkins, and Bill Doyle are some of the writers who honed their craft in Oxford. Marc Smirnoff, who clerked at Square Books, founded the *Oxford-American Magazine* devoted to the best of southern writers. Jamie Kornigay, author of the novel *Soil*, worked there. Lisa Howorth, after having supported and encouraged these writers, became a published fiction writer herself with the novels *Flying Shoes* and *Summerlings*.

Richard and Lisa founded *Thacker Mountain Radio*, a southern version of *Prairie Home Companion* blending music and literature. For over twenty years TMR has entertained and inspired local audiences as well as thousands of listeners on Mississippi Public Radio and recently also Alabama Public Radio. Author Jim Dees hosts the popular weekly program.

If Square Books was the midwife of Oxford's literary revival, Dean was its godmother. Who else in Oxford had gone sailing at Sardis Reservoir with William Faulkner? Who else had grown up playing spot-that-passage at Rowan Oak? Unflagging in her support of belle letters Dean was patron and champion of the growing literary community.

When asked "What's it like to write in the shadow of Faulkner?" Flannery O'Connor famously replied, "Nobody wants his mule and wagon caught on the tracks when the Dixie Express comes through."

Visitors to Oxford often ask if writers in Faulkner's hometown are intimidated or inspired by him. The answer of course is both. Faulkner himself was inspired by Shakespeare and Dostoevski and Proust and James Joyce. He adapted Joyce's stream-of-consciousness technique, took it to new levels, and made it his own. Mr. Bill, as I like to call him, is our guiding star. If we tried to write like Faulkner, it would be too deep a shadow. William Faulkner's tragic vision is Homeric. It is the anvil tone of time. You have to be born with that, and it's both a blessing and a curse. Faulkner's lyrical power, his transcendence, came out of shared pain. He was vein-for-vein immersed in the human tragedy, and with that sensibility and his one-of-a-kind talent he was able to achieve what he did. He said he had no idea where it came from or how it could have happened. Well, it came from inside him. He is the standard bearer. Writers everywhere, but especially those privileged to live and work in Oxford, are ennobled and enabled by his example.

I would add that the scribes of Oxford collectively and consistently nurture the next generation of writers.

As a fledgling newspaper reporter in Philadelphia, Mississippi, in 1983, Sid Salter served as Willie Morris's eyes and ears in compiling material on Marcus Dupree. A year later Sid came to Oxford to share an editorial he had written. I was present at 16 Faculty Row when Willie read Salter's column. He paused to light a cigarette and savor the moment. Salter awaited his verdict, but he knew, and I knew, what Willie would say.

"Damned fine writing!" he told Sid.

Such a benediction from the former editor-in-chief of *Harper's* was the Holy Grail to a young writer, and I saw it happen many times.

Both Morris and Hannah mentored novelist Donna Tartt, who grew up in nearby Grenada. One night Willie showed up at our house with Donna, then a freshman at the university. She possessed a quiet confidence that for one her age was remarkable. Willie and Barry encouraged her to go east and expand her horizons. Tartt wound up at Bennington, where a combination of training and experience led to the composition of her first novel, *The Secret History*.

After a Square Books signing, writers and book lovers often wound up in our kitchen. Jim Dees describes a night when Larry Brown, who as a fireman in 1976 had saved Miss Maud's house from burning, met Jim Harrison.

> *Larry and Dean Faulkner Wells' kitchen table was a warm gathering spot for friends and a touchstone for travelers seeking the Faulkner heat. One such night stands out. The great novelist, essayist and poet, Jim Harrison, was in town for a book conference and he—and half the conference—wound up at Dean and Larry's house. My buddies, Semmes Luckett and Ronzo Shapiro, and I, were ensconced with Jim at the kitchen table where we*

had a relaxed conversation as the party raged around us. The novelist, Larry Brown, a native of Oxford, joined us.

Brown was clearly in awe of Jim and couldn't bring himself to sit with us, preferring to squat on the floor next to the table. He addressed Jim as, "Mr. Harrison." At some point, Brown cleared his throat and began a recitation. "Dear friend now in the dusty clockless hours when the streets lie black and steaming . . ." *We all looked over at him.* ". . . in the wake of water trucks and now when the drunk and homeless have washed up . . ." *It was the opening passage of Cormac McCarthy's novel,* Suttree. ". . . in the lee of walls in alleys or abandoned lots . . ." *Harrison watched with growing bemused respect as Larry spoke without falter.* ". . . and cats go forth highshouldered and lean in the grim perimeters about, now in these sootblacked brick or cobbled corridors where lightwire shadows make a gothic harp of cellar doors . . . no soul shall walk save you."

Larry Brown finished to a round of applause and the image has always stayed with me. Larry squatting on the floor of Miss Maud Faulkner's kitchen, reciting Cormac McCarthy to Jim Harrison. Just part of the everyday magic of 510 South Lamar—a house haunted in a good way.

Dean's first words to Brown when our home was on fire—"*What kept you?*"—would prove prophetic. Brown was then close to publishing his first book, the short story collection *Facing the Music*, which he submitted to Yoknapatawpha Press. We told him that this was a book we would have especially loved to publish, but the timing was terrible. At the time we were suffering seasonal cash flow problems. We advised him to find a publisher on the East Coast, and Algonquin Books in Chapel Hill proved the right fit for him.

In 1988 Willie talked George Plimpton into celebrating the thirty-fifth anniversary of the *Paris Review* in Paris, Mississippi, a hamlet eight miles south of Oxford. Having published a famous interview with Faulkner in 1955, Plimpton instinctively liked the idea, and since he styled himself the commissioner of fireworks for NYC he decided to stage a fireworks show as part of the celebration.

To kick off the thirty-fifth anniversary Dean and I gave a cocktail party in Plimpton's honor. He told us that he had finished writing a screenplay adapting his 1985 novel, *The Curious Case of Sidd Finch*, based on his sensational April Fool's joke for *Sports Illustrated* and ABC News. I recall seeing but not quite believing the ABC news broadcast with its long shot of a man playing a French horn at an isolated beach cottage.

In Plimpton's novel, his hero Sidd Finch, Harvard dropout and wannebe monk, finds inner strength in meditation and music. He builds up his throwing arm in the mountains of Tibet by hurling rocks into space. A Mets baseball scout secretly clocks a Finch fastball at 168 mph.

To develop movie rights Plimpton was researching baseball trivia to lend verisimilitude and help audiences accept Finch as a real person, not Clark Kent with a baseball. Cocktail party conversation turned to whether a 168 mph pitch could be seen, much less caught. Willie Morris opined that the catcher's only option would be to block the pitch with his glove.

"But his hand would probably be broken," he added upon reflection.

It occurred to me that Plimpton might enjoy meeting Jake Gibbs, Ole Miss head baseball coach and former catcher for the Yankees. Who better than Gibbs to speculate on pitches that were too fast to be seen? Plimpton enthusiastically agreed, and I phoned Gibbs.

"Hey, Jake," I said, "would you like to talk to George Plimpton about a 168 mph fastball?" After I explained that Plimpton needed technical advice Gibbs hesitantly agreed to come.

"I don't know if I can help him," Gibbs said, "but I'll be glad to try."

Until that night Dean, Willie, and I had never heard Jake Gibbs discuss the physics of baseball. We had a surprise in store as we introduced the former Yankee to the Paper Lion. Like a flamingo stalking a fish in shallow water Plimpton laid out his scenario.

"How long would the pitch take to reach the catcher?" he said. Jake did not hesitate.

"From the time it left the pitcher's hand," he said, "to when it reached the catcher would take less than a quarter of a second. The catcher could not catch your pitcher's 168 mph fastball, nor could he see it. It would be invisible to the human eye." Ecstatic, Plimpton hastily scribbled every word. Gibbs grinned as he watched George taking dictation. "Coming at you that fast a catcher wouldn't have time to blink," he added, and paused to allow time for Plimpton to write. "I thought I'd heard it all," Jake paused, glancing around at his listeners, "but you never know with these sportswriters!"

"Could a catcher even block a pitch that fast?" Morris said.

"If you had a steel plate in your glove, maybe," Gibbs theorized, "but I wouldn't want to try it, Willie. *Would you?*"

The following night two dozen dinner guests followed Plimpton across the highway from the Paris catfish café where he prepared to light the fuses of the *Paris Review* anniversary fireworks. The chief of the Paris, Mississippi, volunteer fire department informed New York's commissioner of fireworks that the Paris fire department was required by law to supervise a "flammable event."

Plimpton amiably handed over control of the fireworks. And under the aegis of the Paris firefighters, rocket after rocket burst over Yoknapatawpha County, mirroring the energy and vision of *Paris Review* founders Plimpton and Peter Matthiessen.

Later, over a dinner of fried catfish Willie reading from notes scribbled on a napkin referred to the original home of the *Paris Review* as "the other Paris."

Given nights like this it's no wonder that writers were coming out of the woodwork. Shelby Foote once observed that his birthplace, Greenville, Mississippi, had more writers than readers. This was fast becoming true of Oxford as well.

John Grisham funded a guest-writers fellowship at the University of Mississippi. T. R. Pearson was the first writer chosen as a Grisham fellow. When Barry Hannah became director of the Ole Miss creative writing program he tapped a former student at the University of Alabama, Meridian author Brad Watson, to succeed Pearson.

Grisham fellows were lodged at the former home of publisher Seymour Lawrence located on Old Taylor Road half a block from Rowan Oak. Lawrence had purchased the home for his longtime companion Joan Williams, who in the 1950s had been William Faulkner's protégé and paramour. Lawrence further contributed to Oxford's literary revival by donating his private book collection to the University of Mississippi's J. D. Williams Library and endowing a reading room.

Today Oxford is home to a new generation of published authors representing a melting pot of styles and subjects: Curtis Wilkie, Beth Ann Fennelly, Tom Franklin, Jack Pendarvis, Ralph Eubanks, Neil White, Lisa Howorth, Ann Fisher-Wirth, Chris Offutt, Melissa Ginsburg, Ace Atkins, Lee Durkee, Julie Cantrell, Bill Doyle, John T. Edge, Wright Thompson, and Bill Dunlap—among others. Oxford's historians include Charles Eagles, Vaughn Grisham, Kathleen Wickham, and Ellen Meacham. Leading photographers are Alysia Steele, Bruce Newman, Ed Meek, Milly West, Tom Rankin, Ed Croom, and Jane Rule Burdine. And the newcomers keep coming.

In 1993, Square Books and the Center for the Study of Southern Culture established the Conference for the Book, which brought together fiction and nonfiction writers, journalists, poets, artists, publishers, and literary advocates. In 1995, Pat Conroy was the featured author at the conference. Writing for *Vanity Fair*, John Berendt described Conroy's visit:

> [Conroy] paid homage to the great man of southern letters, William Faulkner, by visiting his estate, Rowan Oak. Faulkner's niece, Dean Faulkner Wells, invited Conroy to her own house, the house that had once been her grandmother's,

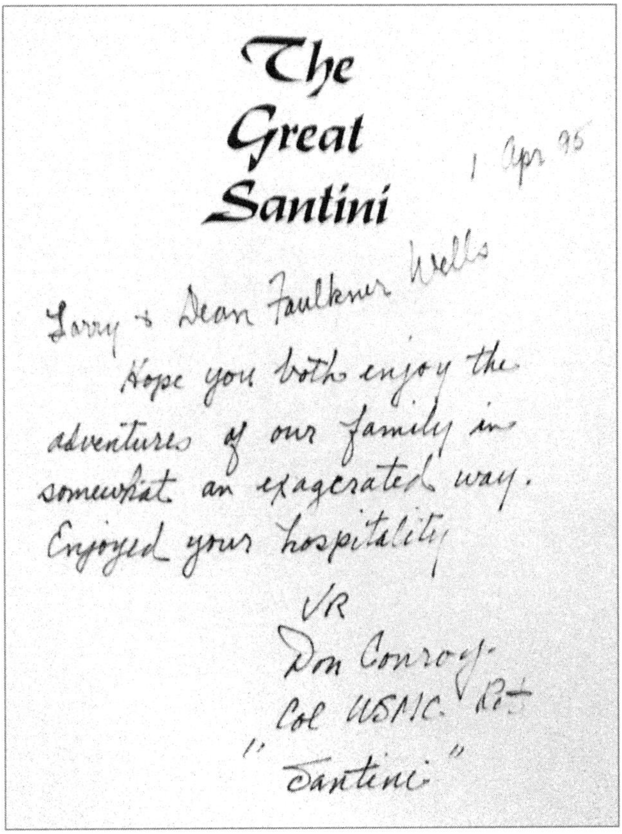
The Great Santini

1 Apr 95

Larry & Dean Faulkner Wells

Hope you both enjoy the adventures of our family in somewhat an exagerated way. Enjoyed your hospitality

VR

Don Conroy

Col USMC Ret

"Santini"

and sat him down at the very table, in the very chair, where Faulkner had completed *Absalom, Absalom!* It was his father, "the Great Santini," who aroused the most curiosity—this man whose violence Conroy had described as "the central fact of my life and art." Don Conroy had become, through his son's books, one of the most hateful father figures in American literature.

Don Conroy indeed had crashed our party, and Pat moved from room to room to avoid his father. When the elder Conroy saw that Pat had inscribed *The Great Santini* to us, he took the liberty of inscribing his son's novel as well.

Conroy showed the Absalom table to his former high school teacher, Eugene Norris, who had introduced him to Faulkner. Norris being briefly overcome by emotion Conroy took him outside. They sat on the front steps. Pat put his arm around Norris's shoulders. Miss Maud's home, which had originally supported a single writer, was becoming a way station for many.

- 23 -

Journalism Rescues Morris

Willie Morris complained, "I cannot bear to look at another pop quiz!" In the beginning he had thrown himself into teaching, reveled in addressing students face to face, and enjoyed the daily routine. Now the excitement had worn off. One year of grading examinations and term papers was all he could take. He asked me to speak to Will Norton about a transfer to the Department of Journalism.

Before the move could take place, Morris got wind of the fact that Vice Chancellor Noyes was miffed over the housing issue. Against my advice he went to the Lyceum to make amends. Later that day while working at the Yoknapatawpha Press office above Sneed's Hardware I heard a familiar heavy tread on the staircase. Morris came in huffing and puffing. From his expression I could guess what happened. "You saw Noyes?"

Willie sat across the desk from me. I reached into a desk drawer for the Jack Daniel's. He accepted a glass of sour mash, lit a cigarette, and exhaled smoke.

"I started to apologize," he said, "and Dr. Noyes said, 'I do what the chancellor tells me.' That's all he said!"

I revealed that Noyes had told me the same thing. "In his classes Noyes used to refer to the Lyceum as the Kremlin," I said. "He wasn't kidding, was he! Will Norton is standing by. Want me to phone him?"

"*Hell yes!*"

I phoned Dr. Norton, who expressed his delight at the prospect of bringing Morris into the Department of Journalism. I put Willie on the phone. He smiled and hung up.

"I have a new title," he said. "Journalist-in-residence."

A few days later I bumped into Hannah at Square Books. When I told him about Willie's change of venue he smiled.

"Yeah," he said.

Morris threw himself into his new teaching position with his usual enthusiasm. He was to teach a feature-writing class in which student essays would be published in a biannual tabloid journal called the *Ole Miss Magazine*. "It will be available to town and campus," he reported to Dean and me at the kitchen table. "And by the way at the bargain price of $1.00 per issue!"

Morris interviewed prospective students. He wanted only the top tier in his class. When the semester began, he taught the class the same way he'd held editorial meetings at *Harper's*, setting up the various departments and discussing ideas for stories. Before he sent the student reporters to gather material, he assigned essays by David Halberstam, Larry L. King, John Corry, and Marshall Frady, which he'd published in *Harper's*. When they were ready to hit the streets and gather material he let them choose their own assignments and accompanied them on fact-finding missions.

At Mr. Levy's Jitney Jungle grocery store on North Lamar he pointed out shoppers stopping in the aisles, talking and laughing, fellow shoppers instead of being irritated striking up secondary conversations. Standing in the aisle, soaking up the atmosphere, Morris jotted a title, "Litany at the Jitney." Always start with a title, he told his student-essayists, who today look back on Morris's class as a pivotal influence.

Willie couldn't resist contributing to the debut issue of the *Ole Miss Magazine*. He wrote a eulogy to "Billy Goat Hill," a grassy knoll behind centerfield in the baseball stadium at the University of Texas, his alma mater. Longhorn outfielders, Willie wrote, had a secret advantage. After practice they carved footholds in the grass allowing them to back-pedal up the hill to catch fly balls.

> I took the same route of my college days, when I drove the long stretch from my Mississippi Delta town to Austin in a vintage black and white Plymouth with dual exhausts. Distant expanses of fields, where the court houses, lazy intersections I once knew, greet me now in the most haphazard déjà vu. Carthage, Palestine, Buffalo, Franklin, Hearne, Rockdale, Thrall—have they existed in a dreamy hush all these years, and awakened now just for me?

The magazine writing-and-publishing class provided an opportunity for Morris to teach by example. From the choice of assignments to his hands-on editing, he passed on invaluable lessons. One night after last call at the Holiday Inn bar, where Morris sometimes convened class (Cokes only for the students, a scholarly ale or two for their professor), he asked me to follow him to 16 Faculty Row. He was eager to show me a mockup of the first issue of the *Ole Miss Magazine*. Curious about what topics he'd assigned, I followed him home. We'd barely sat down when he snatched a felt-tipped pen and started editing.

As long as he was upright, alert, and protected from the elements Willie Morris could edit anywhere, anytime. I watched him transform raw prose into finished product by deleting a word, adding a phrase, pausing now and then to sip bourbon-flavored coffee and weigh the results on his jeweler's scales. Editing, to him, was like breathing, and for a brief time, two semesters, perhaps, the *Ole Miss Magazine* gave him a feeling of being back in the saddle.

Editing for publication with none of the pressures of New York City, he flicked away this digression and that cliché, entered the writer's thought process, and reshaped the narrative without altering style or voice. I was being made privy to the sure instincts of a professional editor. Looking over his shoulder as he worked, blinking away the cigarette smoke, I knew very well that this was *my* editing tutorial under Professor Morris. A quiet satisfaction grew as he worked—not pleasure, exactly, considering this was child's play for him—but a deep contentment. Under his hand the student-essays, some of them awkward and lacking coordination, became as good as they had a right to be. Structure was a common problem, which Morris solved by simply circling a paragraph and drawing an overlapping arrow stretching from one page to another. Grunting to himself, panting fumes, he touched up each essay, some less than others given the writer's ability, leaving style and substance intact. All he added was shading for depth and focus.

Willie knew when to quit. He folded a student paper, creased it down the middle, and said, "Nine down, three more to go." I doubt he was aware that I marveled at how an editor's mind worked, how he tiptoed a fine line between polishing and revision, how I felt deprived when there were no more essays for him to edit.

His influence at the University of Mississippi from 1980 to 1990 can't be overstated. He dispensed advice in bars, bookstores, homes, football stadiums—anywhere a wannabe writer caught him with time on his hands. His canon, I would submit, can be multiplied a hundred-fold by the output of writers he taught. What he showed students over and over was not how to write but how to edit themselves, and that the key is distancing oneself from one's work.

When my novel *Rommel and the Rebel* was published I thanked Willie for teaching me how to edit myself, the last hurdle for any writer. He shrugged and said something I'd heard him tell one of students:

"It was in you all along. Sooner or later it had to come out."

- 24 -

James Dickey

In 1981 Willie Morris invited his old friend, James Dickey, writer-in-residence at the University of South Carolina, to speak at Ole Miss. Dickey had written for *Harper's* when Morris was editor-in-chief. Had I known about their longstanding rivalry, what occurred during Dickey's visit would not have surprised me.

Years earlier, Dickey's wife, Deborah, had saved his life during an alcoholic seizure. From then on, he'd been on the wagon except when outside her jurisdiction. After landing in Memphis he asked the Ole Miss shuttle driver to stop at a 7–11. Between Memphis and Oxford, Dickey polished off six cans of malt liquor.

How does one tell the author of *Deliverance* he's had one too many without taking an arrow to the head?

Morris welcomed Dickey to Oxford, then noting his friend's condition hastily arranged a picnic sans alcohol at a state park. A literary intervention team went into action. Dean, history professor David Sansing, and I went along to entertain and distract Willie's distinguished guest. At Hurricane Landing on Sardis Lake Dickey sipped bottled water and stared gloomily at cypress stumps in the lake. He may have been thinking of the dammed "Cahulawassee River" in *Deliverance*. Willie's plan worked. That afternoon, a sober Dickey gave an informative and entertaining talk at the university library. Afterward, Dean and I gave a one-drink reception at Miss Maud's. Cutting the celebration short, the company repaired to

Taylor Grocery, the same catfish restaurant where we'd taken Morris in 1979.

At a private table for ten, Dickey sipped vodka. Then he turned somberly to his host. "You're living the good life, Willie. Who doesn't like the good life! But there's such a thing as having too much fun. Be thinking about your next book. You owe it to your readers. When are you going to deliver?"

Morris lit a cigarette. He could have brushed aside the remark but chose not to. Who was Dickey to tell him he wasn't producing! To a hushed table he told Dickey, in effect, to mind his own business. Hearing this, one of the dinner guests, a debutante known for her histrionics—Willie had once compared her to Blanche DuBois—burst into artificial tears.

"I can't take this nasty squabbling," she sobbed. "Why can't you boys get along!?"

Dickey hadn't intended to embarrass Willie. To him, this was a typical conversation between writers. *What's on your mind? What are you working on?* But he'd said the right thing at the wrong time. Casting about for distraction he mistook a bowl of tartar sauce for vichyssoise, grabbed a spoon, and gobbled the contents. Everyone saw what was happening but nobody tried to stop him. Within seconds of eating the tartar sauce Dickey groaned, "Somebody take me home." But South Carolina's minister of culture had done his job. He'd prodded Willie to think about his next book.

- 25 -

The Courting of Marcus Dupree

David Halberstam came to Mississippi to celebrate the twenty-fifth anniversary of his first paying job out of Harvard. He'd been hired as a cub reporter by the *Daily Leader* of West Point, Mississippi. After visiting West Point, Halberstam stopped by Oxford to see his former boss at *Harper's*. Our dinner group at the Sizzler included businessman William Lewis and newspaper owner Gale Denley, Morris's colleague in the journalism department. Halberstam told us that in West Point the buzz—and he glanced pointedly at Morris—was about a high school running back named Marcus Dupree.

Halberstam began to tell about Dupree, a gifted athlete, perhaps the greatest running back in the history of Mississippi. I realized immediately that he was gift wrapping a book idea for Willie. Yet the recipient affected not to notice. Perhaps Willie had assumed Halberstam himself was planning to write about Marcus Dupree. I'd heard him complain about sitting in Bobby Van's in Bridgehampton as writers rhapsodized over book deals. "The same old *me-me-me*, all hot air and self-indulgence," he'd said. Maybe the problem was jealousy, I thought, remembering Dickey's recent visit.

The Lewises invited everyone to stop by their home for a nightcap. Once there, Halberstam continued to be the center of attention.

"I'm tired of this literary chit-chat!" Willie exploded. "I heard enough in Bridgehampton to last me two lifetimes. I'm finished with all that. I'm just a simple Mississippi schoolteacher!"

Rocking back and forth in his chair Halberstam hugged himself. What could he say to make amends? As we left the Lewis home, Halberstam, who'd played basketball at Harvard, picked up a loose ball under the goal and trying to lighten the mood started to shoot a layup. He slipped in his penny loafers and fell to the pavement. I was afraid that he'd injured himself but he shook it off. Morris showed little or no concern.

The next morning I came to pick up Halberstam and drive him to Memphis. He was standing in the driveway with his suitcase.

"Willie didn't even say goodnight!" he said. "He sat up all night drinking."

"Don't worry, he'll get over it," I said, opening the trunk to stow his bag. As we got in the car Willie appeared in the driveway, shaggy and sullen, a bear in a red golf shirt. Without a word he got into the backseat. He'd brought a six pack with him. To him beer was a morning drink to tide him over until Bloody Marys.

For thirty minutes we rode in silence, Morris chain-smoking, morose, the picture of gloom. Halberstam returned to the subject of Marcus Dupree, calling him unstoppable, godlike. Willie's massive silence filled the car.

"How good was Marcus Dupree?" I asked, fueling the conversation.

"A man among boys," Halberstam replied. "He can juke a defensive back or run over him."

"How fast is he?"

"Unbelievably fast for a kid that size, six-two, two-twenty-five."

"Are you planning to write about Dupree?"

"No," Halberstam said. I felt the first flicker of Willie's curiosity tickle the back of my neck. Think of a feather tapping *SOS* in Morse code. "I've written enough about sports for a while," David went on, then added for Morris's benefit, "but *someone* should write about Dupree!"

Balloon ascension, Oxford courthouse square, July 4, 1976, Dean F. Wells waving at camera. Photo by Steve Parham.

John Faulkner painting of 1905 Oxford balloon ascension. Photo courtesy of Dianne Falkner.

"*What's a participle?*" Photo of Dean Faulkner Wells. Photo by Susie James.

". . . the eternal process of getting to know each other's past." Photo by Hunter Cole.

"Being allowed to smell the talcum, it seemed to me, was tantamount to receiving Maud's blessing in absentia." Photo of Maud Butler Falkner, c. 1956. Photo courtesy of the Dean and Larry Wells collection.

Wedding reception at Cho Cho's, October 6, 1972. *Left to right*: Vicki, Larry, Dean, and Cho Cho. Photo by Glenn L. Wells Sr.

John, Jimmy, Chooky, and Lucille Faulkner. Photo courtesy of the Dean and Larry Wells collection.

The backward "N" in J. W. T. Falkner's gatestone was enshrined by William Faulkner in his first book, *Marionettes*. Photo by Hunter Cole.

"*Wese*"—Louise Meadow at the Absalom table, c. 1962. Photo by Martin Dain, courtesy of University of Mississippi Archives.

At stake in the twenty-year war between Dean and her mother: residence in Murry and Maud Falkner's home at 510 South Lamar in Oxford. Photo by author.

Miss Maud's famous motto. Photo by author.

Family ghosts: Maud's talcum and William's pipe smoke. Photo by author.

"*. . . an eerie phosphorescence clung to the cedars as if the lightning bugs were in league with the ghosts of Rowan Oak.*" Photo by Murray Riss.

"*Married with children.*" *Left to right*: Dean, Larry, Louise, Dorothy Wells, Jane Wells Scott, and Jon (*bottom right*). Taken shortly before the disastrous rehearsal dinner, October 5, 1972. Photo by Glenn L. Wells Sr.

Larry and Dean at rehearsal dinner. Photo by Glenn L. Wells Sr.

"*We should have jumped the broom.*" Photo by Glenn L. Wells Sr.

With Diane at our wedding reception. Photo by Glenn L. Wells Sr.

William Faulkner: The Cofield Collection. Yoknapatawpha Press, 1978.

"*We backed into the publishing business . . .*" Larry and Dean at the "Gavin Stevens" Yoknapatawpha Press office on the Oxford square. Photo by Chip Cooper.

Lightning fire

A fire at the home of Larry Wells and family was fought by firemen Tuesday afternoon. Lightning struck the west end of the home but the resulting fire was confined to the attic.
—Staff photo by SUSIE

"Home Fires Burning": *Oxford Eagle* coverage of 1976 fire caused by lightning at 510 South Lamar.

Thunderstorm keeps Oxford firemen busy

By ALMA STEAD
Staff Writer

Oxford's firemen responded to eight calls yesterday, four of them within 20 minutes during a thunderstorm.

Mrs. Hazeltine Gooden's house 1415 Washington Ave., was struck by lightning twice, once at 5:30 and again at 8:49. The first time a switchbox caught on fire, catching bedding stored in the same room with it, and causing soot damage to clothing. The second time no fire was started, but as a precaution the electric power to the house was cut off. No one was hurt. Two trucks answered each call.

The home of Larry Wells at 510 South Lamar was struck by lightning at 5:14. Fire department officials said the fire was visible at the west end of the house when they got there. They estimated $1000 to $1500 worth of damage. Two engines and 18 men answered this call.

A dwelling on old highway 6 west was struck by lightning at 5:13. One truck and two men answered this call.

Lightning apparently struck the residence of Gordon Baird on Vivian, but no damage was caused. One truck and two men answered this call at 5:37.

At 7:40 Mrs. Pearl Beck's residence on Highway 7 North was struck by lightning in a switchbox. Two men and one truck responded to the call.

At 9:16 a storage shed at the residence of Russell Aven on Park Drive was struck by lightning. Two trucks and seven men responded.

At 9:20 a smoke smell was reported behind the Beacon Restaurant. One truck and two men checked it out and found that the smoke was drifting over from the Aven shed.

Sage motto

Sage motto written by her grandmother in her hands, Dean Faulkner Wells and daughter watch firemen extinguish the fire in their home, one of several fires started by lightning during the sudden electric storm which struck Oxford Tuesday afternoon and evening.
—Staff photo by SUSIE

Dean and her daughter Paige. Note the "Don't Complain, Don't Explain" sign Dean is holding.

"*What to save? The children.*" *Left to right*: Jon, Larry, Lawrence, Paige, Catherine, and Diane. Photo by Glenn L. Wells Sr.

Dean, Vicki, and Larry at 1978 Greenwood Arts Festival prior to meeting Willie Morris. Photo courtesy of the Dean and Larry Wells Collection.

Willie's "scouting trip" to Oxford, October 1979. *Left to right*: Larry, Willie, Dean, and Adam Shaw. Photo by Walt Mixon.

"*WILLIE*"—Willie Morris with his dog Pete, the "mayor of Bridgehampton," 1980. Photo by Susie James.

The Ghosts of Rowan Oak, Yoknapatawpha Press, 1980. Cover illustration by John F. Davis.

Dean writing *The Ghosts of Rowan Oak* at the Absalom table, 1980. Photo by author.

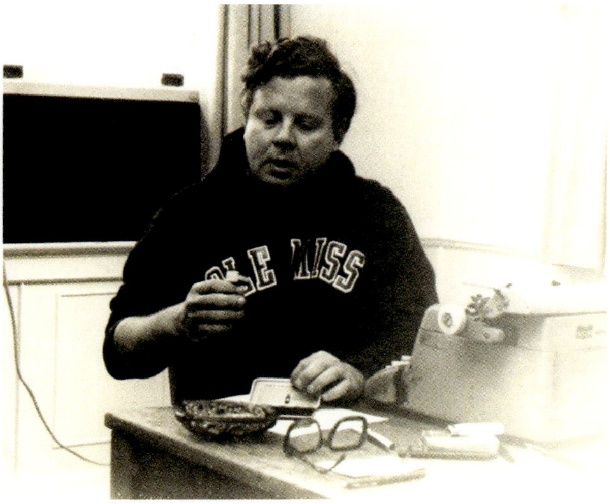

Willie, forty-six, moved into #16 Faculty Row at Ole Miss in 1980. Photo by Kathy Ferguson.

Good Old Boy, Yoknapatawpha Press, 1980. Cover design by William Lester.

"*We were all running away from something . . .*" At Bobby Van's in Bridgehampton, New York. *Left to right*: the author, Bobby Van, Marina Van, and Dean. Photo from the author's collection.

Bobby Van's in Bridgehampton. Photo courtesy of Bobby Van's.

"*Are You from Dixie?*" Songsters Larry Wells, Jenny Baldwin, and John Davis. Photo by unknown.

Willie Morris at the Holiday Inn bar. Photo by Alen MacWeeney.

Willie and his dog Pete, who died in 1983. Photo by David Rae Morris.

In 1988 Willie talked George Plimpton into celebrating the thirty-fifth anniversary of the *Paris Review* in Paris, Mississippi, located eight miles south of Oxford. *Left to right*: William Styron, Willie Morris, and George Plimpton. Photo by Bruce Newman.

"*I could overpower you and take your woman.*" Barry Hannah on the Oxford square. Photo © by Maude Schulyer Clay.

"*Rivals-in-residence*" Willie Morris with Barry Hannah at 1990 engagement party for Willie and JoAnne Prichard. Photo by John Morgan.

"*You can't change who you are, so relax and enjoy the ride,*" Peets Buffett told Dean. *Left to right*: Jimmy, Peets, and Lucy Buffett. Photo courtesy of Buffett family.

Left to right: Oxford writers: Curtis Wilkie, Neil White, Megan Abbott, Beth Ann Fennelly, Ace Atkins, Tom Franklin, Julie Cantrell, Ann Fisher-Wirth, and Larry Wells. Photo by Bruce Newman.

Dean's fiftieth birthday party at the Hoka, 1986. *Left to right*: Jim Dees, Dean, Ron Shapiro, Willie Morris. Photo by Barney Sellers, *Mid-South Magazine*, courtesy of the *Commercial Appeal*.

Ron Shapiro's Hoka Theatre in Oxford. Photo by Keith Gore Wiseman.

Willie Morris at the world premiere of the Disney movie of *Good Old Boy*. Photo from Vernon Richards film.

Arriving at the Hoka for the premiere are Jon Mallard with his dog "Denver" at the wheel, Billy Chadwick, and honoree Willie Morris. Photo courtesy of Ron Shapiro.

Barry Hannah and Willie Morris being interviewed before the movie debut. Photo from Vernon Richards film.

Ron Shapiro at *Good Old Boy* premiere. Photo courtesy of Vernon Richards.

Willie on the way to movie wrap party in Natchez, 1989. Photo by author.

"*Larry and Dean's kitchen table was a warm gathering spot for friends and a touchstone for travelers seeking the Faulkner heat.*" *Left to right*: Semmes Luckett, Jim Harrison, Jim Dees, and Ron Shapiro. Photo courtesy of Ron Shapiro.

Square Books staff. *Left to right*: Lisa Howorth, Richard Howorth, Cody Morrison, Lyn Roberts, and Slade Lewis. Photo © by Maude Schuyler Clay.

Square Books by Glennray Tutor.

The "Dean Faulkner Wells" impostors at the Lyric Theatre, *left to right*: Jack Pendarvis, Larry and Dean, Lee Durkee, Ace Atkins, Wright Thompson, and Tom Franklin. Photo by Bruce Newman.

Every Day by the Sun, Crown Publishing Group, 2011.

"*I'm Dean.*" Standing ovation for Dean at Oxford's Lyric Theatre at 2011 book launch of her memoir, *Every Day by the Sun*. Photo by Bruce Newman.

This was my cue. "Look where it's set, in Philadelphia, Mississippi, where Chaney, Schwerner, and Goodman were murdered!" The civil rights trio were killed in 1964 during Freedom Summer. It took decades for those responsible to be brought to justice.

As if with a bullhorn Halberstam plugged the project, "An African American running back is helping bring whites and blacks together in Philadelphia, Mississippi, city of Brotherly Love!"

"Willie was born to write this book," I added.

Finally from the backseat a cry of hope. "*This will be a fucking great book!*"

By the time we reached Memphis Airport Willie was talking about negotiating a book deal. "How much do you think Sterling could get me?"

"A hundred grand," Halberstam said confidently. "All you'd need for an auction is a two-page summary."

"Two pages," Morris sighed. This was a book he couldn't have written *unless* he had come back to Mississippi. It was all part of a piece: Halberstam's anniversary celebration in West Point, Willie's outburst at the Lewises', David desperate to make up for the imagined slight, and writers' shoptalk on the way to Memphis. Halberstam and Morris shook hands.

"The title will be 'The Courting of Marcus Dupree,'" Willie said.

During his ten-year sojourn in Bridgehampton he had written *James Jones, A Friendship*, and *The Last of the Southern Girls*. In Oxford he'd produced a new collection of essays, *Terrains of the Heart*, for Yoknapatawpha Press, which he'd dedicated to Dean and me. Now Morris gathered himself to write his first full-length book since moving to Mississippi. He'd waited patiently for original material to come to him and intended to make the most of the opportunity. He began by stocking up on felt-tipped pens and legal pads, and putting a new ribbon in his typewriter. Then he cut back on his drinking.

That fall he drove south every Friday to see Marcus Dupree play football. David Sansing and I accompanied him to a game in the town of Ackerman. Before the game we paid a call on the former Mississippi governor James P. Coleman, who took us into a separate building and showed off his complete set of "War of the Rebellion: Official Records of the Union and Confederate Armies" (128 vols.) and "War of the Rebellion: Official Records of the Union and Confederate Navies" (31 vols.). Professor Sansing observed that the collection was "doubtless headed for a museum."

I glanced at Willie to see if he was thinking the same thing I was, that the enclosed, one-room building was dedicated to the "Lost Cause." We were knee deep in a political riptide. The trail to Marcus Dupree led through Governor Coleman's Confederate library. Coleman represented traditional conservative values whereas Willie represented the New South. I could almost hear Willie thinking, "When was Mississippi *not* tormented by its past?"

If anyone understood the complexities of this tortured state it was Morris. He'd come to write about how a talented black athlete was bringing whites and blacks together in Philadelphia, which had been a death trap for three civil rights workers. Now, in this museum to the Old Confederacy, Willie's Yazoo City boyhood and southern manners forced him to pay lip service to an ex-governor who created the State Sovereignty Commission and prevented Clennon Washington King Jr. from entering the University of Mississippi in 1958.

Surrounded by tomes defending Mississippi's Confederate past Morris was sweating from every pore. It's difficult to explain to northerners or Europeans how a right-minded southerner can be loyal to conservative friends while remaining liberal. Like every white person who grew in the segregated South, Morris had been programmed to accept the status quo. Not until he left Mississippi did he learn the lyrics to "We Shall Overcome."

Willie's magnum opus, *North Toward Home*, had given thousands of white southerners hope and resolve. A Mississippian, one of their own, had demonstrated that guilt and shame were a part of growing up white in the South, that no matter how blue the sky, how brilliant the sunshine, those who ignored the lessons of history were doomed to repeat it, and that the only way to deal with intolerance and injustice was to speak out against it.

A scant two hours after being surrounded by Coleman's "War of the Rebellion" collection Morris, Sansing, and I sat in the stands at Ackerman High School football stadium as an excited crowd of whites and blacks yelled with one voice, "*Go, Marcus, go!*" Marcus Dupree was running before the winds of change, and Willie was the eye of the hurricane.

The courting of Marcus Dupree started before football season ended. Motels in Philadelphia had no vacancies. Coaches from the SEC, SWC, and Big 12 competed to offer Marcus a scholarship. An assistant coach at Ole Miss slipped Morris inside information about the bidding war. A young Sid Salter introduced Willie to Marcus Dupree. Later back in Oxford, Morris asked his friends to meet him at the Hoka. He needed a code name for his Ole Miss informant.

"Deep Throat is taken," he said, sipping unspiked coffee. "What pseudonym can I give him?"

"How about 'Temple Drake'?" I suggested, referring to Faulkner's amoral central character in *Sanctuary*.

"That's it, boss. That's it!" said Morris, pounding the table.

All that spring Willie talked and talked about *The Courting of Marcus Dupree*. We soon began to worry that he was talking out the book. Sure enough, when summer rolled around he failed to meet Doubleday's deadline. One evening he phoned us, distraught.

"Pete is lying in the front . . . in the front yard!" he groaned. "My Petey wants to die. I made him a bed of leaves. Petey, my poor Petey!"

It rained the day of Pete's funeral. Morris insisted that Pete be buried in St. Peter's Cemetery. Like most states Mississippi had a law against animal burials in human cemeteries. Mayor John Leslie, who did everything he could for Willie, sent a backhoe operator to dig a shallow grave near a discontinued cemetery entrance. Billy Ross Brown built a plywood coffin. Six or seven of Willie's friends turned out for Pete's burial. We gathered around the grave under a steady downpour. Oblivious to the elements Willie stood bareheaded, cupping a lit cigarette and sobbing inconsolably as the plywood box was lowered into the earth. Dean had selected a service in the 1928 *Book of Common Prayer* for the burial of a child. Pete, too, had died without sin.

Rain drummed on umbrellas as Willie wept in a steady tremolo. I read from Dean's white, leather-bound *Book of Common Prayer*:

> Therefore are they before the throne of God and serve him day and night in his temple: and he that is on the throne shall dwell among them. They shall hunger no more, neither thirst anymore, neither shall the sun light on them nor any heat; for the lamb which is in the midst of the throne shall feed them and shall lead them into living fountains of waters, and God shall wipe away all tears from their eyes. [Revelation 7:15]

Pete's honorary pallbearers and Dean—Willie-altar-guild of one—gave Pete a proper wake at the Sizzler. Each of us brought brown paper bags of bourbon and bardolino. Willie wept as he ordered the "Billy Ross Brown special," a ten-ounce New York strip, which ordinarily he wrapped in a napkin for Pete. That night he left his steak untouched.

After dinner we went to the Holiday Inn for a nightcap. Dean begged off. In our all-male group Willie withdrew into himself. We tried to cheer him up with small talk: sporting odds, real estate deals gone wrong, an emergency room physician caught having sex with a nurse.

"Last call," said Clyde, the bartender, hands folded in respect. Willie ordered a Black Russian.

Ed Morgan spoke up, "Boys, we all have to die sometime. Billy Ross, would you take seventy-five if I offered it to you right now?" Brown shrugged. Morgan pressed him, "Yeah, we all want to live a long time, but what if I could guarantee you seventy-five years of life right now? Would you take it!" He began to auction off projected ages of death. When a number was called one of us, amused and tentative, raised his hand. "Seventy-five, going once, going twice. *Sold* to Billy Ross Brown. Seventy-four? Who'll take seventy-four? *Sold* to Charles Henry! Seventy-three, going once, going twice. *Sold* to Ed Perry!" Each accepted Morgan's bargain with death while stealing glances at Morris. When Morgan said, "Who'll take seventy-two?" I obliged by raising my hand. Willie turned on me in contempt. "Seventy-two? Boss, *you* are going to live for a very long time." The Irish in me knew a curse when I heard it, but I put the strange, disparaging remark down to grief.

For a week Morris didn't go out or answer the phone. The silence at 16 Faculty Row was destroying him. Then we heard that he had taken a room at the Holiday Inn. Fortunately, that was the week that *The Winds of War*, the TV mini-series based on Herman Wouk's novel, premiered. Morris phoned us raving about the series. He was in recovery mode but with cash running out couldn't afford to stay at the Holiday Inn any longer.

"What am I going to do?" he asked. "I can't go home with Petey gone!"

Willie's pal, state representative Ed Perry, came up with a solution. He reserved a state park cabin at Sardis Lake. Morris moved in, swore off bourbon, and got down to business.

On October 1, 1983, Doubleday published *The Courting of Marcus Dupree*. A week later Marcus Dupree became involved in a squabble with head coach Barry Switzer, quit the University of Oklahoma football team, and went into hiding. *Where is Marcus Dupree?* screamed the headlines. Reporters from around the nation descended on 16 Faculty Row. Had Marcus reached out to his James Boswell?

Willie had no idea where Marcus had gone but he loved the attention. With all the national publicity Doubleday's first printing of 40,000 would surely sell out in a few weeks. I doubt he slept more than five hours the whole time Dupree was in hiding. As each visitor entered Willie's living room an initiation took place. Willie would place his finger to his lips and the novice would freeze, whispering, "You mean, Marcus is *here*?"

Morris would nod in the direction of his bedroom. Each newcomer made sign language for *May I have a peek?* Fellow reporters looked on, bemused and a bit bored. When the newcomer eased the bedroom door open the assembled sportswriters exploded in mirth, Morris nodding in mild satisfaction.

At week's end Dupree emerged from hiding. He'd been staying in the Mississippi College dorm room of a high school teammate. I was at 16 Faculty Row when Morris phoned his editor, Carolyn Blakemore, to see if the first printing had sold out. To his horror Blakemore told him there had been a "glitch" in the system. The shipping department hadn't received the editorial department's order to release the book. While Marcus was on the run *The Courting of Marcus Dupree* had languished in a Garden City warehouse. The Weird Sisters of Fate had closed ranks against Willie. He said goodbye, replaced the receiver, and lit a cigarette. "Fuck it!" he said.

The Courting of Marcus Dupree sold well but never became the bestseller it could have been, given the national headlines. When the book was officially out of print Willie offered second-edition rights to Yoknapatawpha Press. I wish we'd taken him up on it.

IV. Literary Community

- 26 -

Willie's 50th

Two weeks before November 29, 1984, Willie began dropping hints that his fiftieth birthday was coming up. We were keeping the surprise party a secret. Willie began to fret and fume. The hints became broader. Then he stopped speaking and holed up at 16 Faculty Row.

Meanwhile, birthday planning went forward. Patty and William Lewis were to host the event at Shadow Lawn, their antebellum home. With its central entrance hall and grand staircase, it was the ideal setting. Willie's surprise guests would descend the steps, one at a time, while the birthday boy waited at the foot of the stairs. Flying in from New York and Long Island were Jack Whitaker, Gloria Jones, Rose Styron, Jean Stein, Carolyn Blakemore, Sterling Lord, and Larry L. King. Coming from Alabama were Winston Groom and Peets Buffett. Willie's fellow Rhodes scholar Ed Yoder sent a poem to be read at the party.

Barry Hannah didn't make the guest list due to his refusal to apologize to Dean over a stupid remark.

This latest Hannah misadventure took place during a happy occasion, Diane's upcoming marriage to Michael Cawley, of Orange, Connecticut, our designated driver-in-law and family tennis pro.

Dean had planned an outdoor wedding reception at Rowan Oak. There was just one catch. The federal government which had designated Rowan Oak a national landmark and was partially funding its upkeep prohibited the use of alcohol. I told Howard Bahr, then-curator of Rowan Oak, "Faulkners are genetically incapable of getting married without alcohol. What are we going to do?" Howard laid a finger against his nose and said, "I'll be inside the house receiving visitors." What went on in the garden was none of his business.

"Thanks, Howard!" I said.

Dean appointed Willie official reception spike-meister. A week before the wedding, sitting in his favorite kitchen chair, he laid out his plan. Since we'd be skirting federal law by serving alcohol at Rowan Oak, he planned to mix rum and fruit punch in an empty five-gallon apple juice jug he'd found at the Hoka. "No one will know!" he exclaimed.

From the street outside came a screech of brakes. Every time Hannah saw Willie's car parked at the Chevron, he stopped to see what was going on. He burst into the house and rushed into the kitchen. When he saw his rival-in-residence at the kitchen table he reverted to character—that is to say, his chauvinist fictional character who roamed Central Park with a sawed-off shotgun—and snapped at Dean, "Fix me a drink, you stupid fucking bitch!"

It was like the moment the lightning struck and I smelled smoke. Grimly biting off each word, Dean said, "Bitch I admit to. Fucking is just an expletive. But stupid? *Never! You're out of here!*" She jerked a thumb over her shoulder saying, "Larry, throw him out!"

Hannah pleaded, "I was only kidding."

How was it that Hannah could get away with groping her in the backseat but calling her stupid crossed the line? Of course, the mother of the bride did not have to explain herself and especially one who was standing under her grandmother's "Don't Explain, Don't Complain" sign.

I gave Hannah a shrug as if to say, sorry, the writing is literally on the wall. He stuttered, "The F-f-faulkners have no s-s-sense of humor!" Assuming a bland expression Morris sipped JD and waited to see his rival thrown out. In a daze Barry followed me up the hallway. Dean stuck her head around the door.

"Until *he* apologizes," she called after us, using third-person like a mallet, "*he* will not be welcome."

Up the hallway we went, round and round as if waltzing.

"The Faulkners are too s-s-serious," Barry wheezed. "Read Faulkner's novels and let me know if you find any humor. You won't . . . won't find . . . anything f-f-funny because F-f-faulkner has no s-s-sense of humor!"

Faulkner of course had a terrific sense of humor but at the moment my job was that of bouncer.

Willie's fiftieth birthday party took place on November 29, 1984. We invited him over for "a birthday drink." He knew immediately that his dream was coming true. He entered Miss Maud's house wearing a hopeful expression. Dean admitted that we'd planned drinks with friends at the Lewis's. Willie brightened. Something was afoot. As we escorted him around the corner to the Lewis home he spotted an overflow crowd in the yard. Beaming in anticipation he strode up the cedar-lined walk.

Well-wishers surrounded him and escorted him inside where David Rae Morris, acting as emcee, stationed his father at the foot of the stairs, and introduced the out-of-towners. Appearing one by one on the second-story landing, Willie's friends paraded down the stairs into his embrace. I presented him with a poem by Ed Yoder.

We'd hired a photographer, the resulting birthday album to be signed by guests. The entourage mounted up and rode to (where else?) the Sizzler, which Sparky Reardan and Dean's daughter Diane had decorated with balloons and streamers.

During the meal, songs and skits were performed by Willie's friends. A Yazoo City quartet—Bubba and Lou Mott, Herman and Harriet Decell—sang a song they composed for the occasion. Gloria Jones, Rose Styron, Patty Lewis, and Jean Stein sang Willie's favorite song, "As Time Goes By." Willie was busy making napkin-notes for his thank-you's. The planners having forgotten to order a cake, Dean and Rose stuck a candle in a cheesecake, and everyone sang "Happy Birthday."

"I'd like to thank my cheesecake team," Willie began his after-dinner remarks. "Starring Rose Styron at halfback, Gloria Jones at fullback, and that all-star southern quarterback, Deanie Faulkner Wells!"

And so the Willie Morris Society of Oxford and New York ushered their beloved Willie into a new decade. Ronald Reagan was president. *The Sicilian* by Mario Puzo headed the *New York Times* bestseller list. November 29, 1984, was Liberation Day in Albania. And the number-one song on the charts was "Wake Me Up before You Go-Go," by Wham!

Willie was born under the Centaur constellation. A Sagittarius always maintains a positive outlook on life. He is profoundly curious, energetic, optimistic, and enthusiastic. He enjoys meeting new people and has a vibrant personality but can often be reckless.

- 27 -

Playing Games

I SWALLOWED A YAWN, MADE MY APOLOGIES, AND HOPED WILLIE would take the hint. It was nearly two a.m. on a Sunday night, but he didn't care any more than a two-year-old that at six-thirty Dean would be cooking breakfast for the kids and preparing school lunches. He'd started playing word games, his last delaying tactic to keep from having to leave. Being a night owl Dean could function on less sleep than I could. I gave up when the town clock struck two, said goodnight, and retired.

The next morning I asked Dean what happened. She was ironing a dress for Paige at the time.

"We played finish the quote," she said. "Turning and turning in the widening gyre—"

The falcon cannot hear the falconer.

"Then we played guess the college mascot. What's the name of the Delaware team?"

Blue hens.

"University of South Dakota?"

That's hard.

"Coyotes. At two-thirty, we matched fictional characters with book titles. At two-forty-five we named the US presidents. At three he asked if I knew the infield fly rule. Then he demanded pencil and paper and started planning his funeral. He made a list of speakers starting with William Styron, George Plimpton, and

David Halberstam. The wake was to go on for a month. He asked me to bring pound cake."

And a bottle of Jack Daniel's?

"Yes."

And before you could ask him to leave, he begged you to plan your funeral.

"Yes, I want a simple graveside service with Vivaldi's 'Four Seasons' played by a string quartet. All present are to sing 'Ding, dong, the Witch is Dead!'" She continued, "We discussed what poems would be read over us. I took out an anthology of southern literature and found Wallace Stevens's 'Sunday Morning.' You know my favorite stanza."

We live in an old chaos of the sun,
Or old dependency of day and night,
Or island solitude, unsponsored, free,
Of that wide water, inescapable.
Deer walk upon our mountains, and the quail
Whistle about us their spontaneous cries;
Sweet berries ripen in the wilderness;
And, in the isolation of the sky,
At evening, casual flocks of pigeons make
Ambiguous undulations as they sink,
Downward to darkness, on extended wings.

Courtly love is like jazzercise. It keeps everyone including sleeping husbands on their toes. Having played similar word games at Rowan Oak, Dean delighted in Willie's prodigious memory and playful sense of humor. Like her, Willie grew up an only child and a social animal. He had become the brother she never had. But even so, she wasn't sitting up half the night for her own amusement. All her life she'd wondered if she were loved for herself and not for her uncle's fame. She needed Willie's assurances that her character and personality were what mattered, not her bloodline. Yet no matter how late she allowed him to stay, he always left in a huff, slamming the screened door on his way out.

The trouble began when I was commuting to Alabama bookstores selling *Legend in Crimson*, a photo-history of University of Alabama football. One night I got back to Oxford around nine p.m. I'd been on the road all day and was tired. Willie dropped by for cocktails and offered to buy dinner.

"If we hurry we can get to the Sizzler before they stop serving," he said, eager as a puppy. "I've got bourbon and wine."

"One drink in my present condition would put me to sleep," I said. But Willie wouldn't take no for an answer. Reluctantly I agreed. Dean had consumed more wine than usual and needed food.

When we arrived at the Sizzler the owners Bill and Gladys Sparks were turning out the lights. They dutifully opened the kitchen and prepared steaks and salad at warp speed. Halfway through the meal Dean asked where my daughter Catherine wanted to go to college.

"When the time comes Catherine will make up her own mind," I said. "It's a ways off, yet."

Dean began pushing Millsaps while Willie rather aggressively promoted Sewanee, the University of the South. It felt like the tag-team tactics of Vicki and Cho Cho when I drove them to Oxford from Memphis. I repeated that Catherine would make her choice and I was satisfied to let her. To my surprise Dean made an Alamo-like stand. It had to be Millsaps. I clammed up. It was time to finish the meal and let Bill and Gladys close the restaurant.

With nods and winks Willie let Dean know that he was on her side. Emboldened, two against one, she turned to me with a scathing look: "Are you afraid that Catherine can't get into Millsaps?"

"What's the matter with you?" I said and held up my hand as though to shield myself from her scorn. To my surprise she threw wine in my face and stormed out of the restaurant. I knew immediately that this was a "don't explain" moment and that she'd never tell me why she did it. Willie lit a cigarette and waited to see what happened next. Behind the counter Bill and Gladys tried not to stare. Wiping off the wine I went to see about Dean.

By the time I emerged from the roadhouse she had disappeared. I got in the car and went looking for her. Moments later the headlights illuminated a small, erect figure marching on the shoulder of the highway. She looked so small and fragile. I felt terrible about the blowup. Driving on the shoulder of the road I slowly followed her. Oncoming traffic slowed down as drivers gawked at the sight of a car trailing a woman on foot.

"For Christ's sake, get in!" I called out the window. "You can't walk six miles back to town." I got out and tried walking after her. She whirled around stretching out her hands.

"You . . . I'm going to tear up our marriage license when I get home," she yelled.

A threat uttered under the influence was best ignored. I returned to the car, drove back to the Sizzler, and gave Willie the keys. He was more than willing to play knight in shining armor.

Later I found out that when Dean reached the top of the hill she stopped to catch her breath. The white Oldsmobile crept past but in the dark Willie didn't spot her.

"*Willie!*" she shouted as loud as she could. Despite passing dozens of driveways and intersections he couldn't decide where to pull off and drove the full six miles to Oxford before turning around.

She waited at the top of the next hill, failing to notice that a Labrador retriever from a nearby farmhouse had crept up beside her. It took her wrist in its mouth.

"Nice doggie," she said. "Nice doggie!" Having owned a Lab she was confident it wouldn't bite her if she didn't try to get away. She stood very still praying that Willie would find her. At the foot of the hill I sat on the Sizzler steps praying just as hard that Dean wouldn't carry out her threat to tear up our marriage license. We'd been married fifteen years without a public squabble.

Once, walking home from a football game, Dean accused me of having married her because she was Pappy's niece. Nothing could have been further from the truth. "We were friends before we were lovers," I said, "and Pappy had nothing to do with either."

Now, another shadow was hanging over us. Had Willie influenced her outburst at the Sizzler? Without his subtle encouragement would she have lost her temper over a pointless argument and thrown wine in my face?

Over the past four years our relationship with Willie had become more and more incestuous. Not only had we reissued *Good Old Boy* and *North Toward Home* but we were planning to publish a collection of his sports stories entitled *Always Stand In against the Curve.* We'd become not only his publishers but in a real sense his foster family. Hanging out together as a threesome couldn't go on forever. It was time Willie found a home of his own.

A screech of tires shattered the stillness. In the dark Willie had missed the Sizzler's driveway and was backing up. I thanked him and took the wheel. We rode back to town in silence. Satisfaction was coming off him in waves. What was there to say? This senseless, drunken spat was best forgotten. At Willie's request, I dropped him off at the Holiday Inn.

When I got home, Dean met me in the hallway. We both apologized at the same time.

"You were tired and needed peace and quiet," she said.

"And you put in a full day at the office," I added.

"And drank far too much wine," she said. "But that's no excuse for what happened." Coming from the woman who never explained this was the Gettysburg address.

"I was scared to death a car was going to hit you," I said.

We held hands on the way to bed.

After the Sizzler blowup Willie went on a self-imposed diet. Gradually Dean and I realized that he'd stopped drinking bourbon, gin, and vodka, limiting himself to only wine and beer. Maybe he'd noticed that in the provinces, as he referred to Mississippi, appearances mattered. People noticed if his pants were split at the seam, or if he forgot to wear socks, or sweated into sofas and stained the upholstery.

"Oh, that Willie!" gossipers laughed behind his back. Typically, he gave scant credence to such blather, but of late he'd decided to improve his appearance. For two months he refrained from drinking whiskey, exercised in a rubber suit, and sweated off the pounds. If we didn't know better we'd have thought he was getting into courting shape. Who, we wondered, was the lucky lady?

One day, needing a signature on a contract I went to 16 Faculty Row. Willie had just gotten back from a power walk. The top half of his rubber suit peeled back from his tummy like a bell. As he signed the papers I heard what sounded like rain. I looked down. Sweat drops danced in a circle around Willie's feet. When he walked into an adjoining room he left a puddle trail.

By the end of August he was fit and trim.

One weekend I left to attend a family reunion in Alabama. That evening around six p.m. Dean heard a knock at the door. There stood Willie with a bouquet of red roses. He was clean-shaven with a knick here and there. He wore a blazer and tie. Willie never put on a tie unless he absolutely had to. This meant trouble. She almost sent him away but didn't have the heart.

"What is it, Willie?" she said. He pulled at his collar, then spoke through the screen.

"Deanie," he said, "love me once before I die."

It was like her ex-boyfriend, the bank president, showing up in courting mode, except this time our friendship with Willie was on the line. Reluctantly she let him in. Penny loafers scuffing the hardwood floor he followed her to the kitchen. She filled two glasses of wine half-full. This was no time to lose her wits. She was grateful for comforting sounds of Jaybird practicing free throws in the driveway. He could sink twenty-five in a row. As he prepared to take a shot he dribbled three times. The *thump, thump, thump* of the basketball was like the beating of her heart. She chose her words carefully.

"Willie," she said, "you are the brother I never had." Jaybird dribbled between shots. He never deviated from the routine. *One, two, three . . . swoosh.* "The fight Larry and I had at the Sizzler didn't mean anything." A restaurant argument didn't signal the end of a marriage. She hoped Willie understood.

All those Sunday nights, the parlor games and wine and laughter, had been leading up to this moment. Dean adored writers this side of idolatry. What Willie failed to acknowledge was that she'd married one.

"I think you'd better go, Willie," she added, hoping that in the days to come if he didn't remember anything else, he'd remember her tone of voice.

Grinding his cigarette in an ashtray Willie tossed the bouquet on the table and left the kitchen. Relieved and contrite Dean followed him up the hallway. He did not slam the screen door as usual but eased it shut. That, too, was sad.

"Larry is your friend!" she called after him. Willie gave no sign that he heard. She returned to the kitchen, called Jaybird in, and asked him to take the roses to his grandmother.

That evening I returned from Alabama. When Dean told me what had happened my initial reaction was relief. This scene had been building from the moment we met Willie. I was glad it was over. "Now we can move on," I said, hoping that Willie would see the light.

Tired from the long drive I stripped off my clothes and drew a bath. Hearing a commotion in the yard I looked out the bedroom window. Drunk and belligerent, fists clenched, shirt loose over his trousers Willie bellowed for me to come out. He must have seen my car in the driveway. His slurred voice indicated that he'd fallen off the wagon.

"Willie, what's the matter?" Dean called through the screened door. Passing motorists slowed down to stare. A forelock hanging over his forehead Willie searched for an excuse.

"I won't have my new book priced so high!" he cried in a shrill, petulant tone. "Thirteen ninety-five is highway robbery. I'm embarrassed for my friends to pay so much."

We'd set the preliminary price of *Always Stand In against the Curve* at thirteen dollars and ninety-five cents, a then-normal price for an illustrated trade hardcover. I came into the hallway with a towel around my waist.

"Willie, that's not it," Dean called. "What in the world is the matter?"

Her instinct was to protect Willie from gossip just as she'd protected Barry's reputation the night he groped her. A writer had to be saved from his own impulses. Asking her to run away with him was one thing. Making a fool of himself in front of God and Oxford was another.

"Send him out!" Morris repeated though with less conviction, kicking at the grass.

Dean had gotten us into this mess. It was up to her to get us out. What she did next was sheer genius.

"*Willie!*" she scolded in a preemptory but playful way. "What's the capital of Missouri?"

He stared as if his heart were a fence with a plank missing. She was giving him a chance to laugh at himself. If he failed to live up to her expectations he was not the man she thought he was.

One night while sitting up with Willie she'd asked him to read from his prize-winning memoir *North Toward Home*. She took the book off the living room shelf and on the way to the kitchen noticed his inscription. "*To Deanie and Larry, Around the kitchen table from here to eternity, Willie.*" She returned to the kitchen and told him that when she read this autobiography nearly two decades ago, he had her instant respect, admiration, and love. Apparently Willie heard only the last word.

Like a johnny jump-up blooming overnight, the printer's deadline for *Always Stand In against the Curve* arrived. I left a note in Willie's car asking him to proofread the jacket copy. It was the perfect way for us to make peace. We met at the Holiday Inn bar, which, at the hotel manager's request, Willie had christened the "Prince Albert Room." We shook hands and sat down together. He ordered bourbon. I ordered beer. To say that we were wary of each other is an understatement.

I wasn't angry at him for making a run at Dean. In retrospect it was inevitable. Once, at a football game at Birmingham's Legion Field, one of my cousins who'd just met Dean innocently asked, "Oh, are you from Mississippi?" Whereupon my uncle Eric McGee said, "Honey, she *is* Mississippi."

Why wouldn't Willie adore her? There would be something wrong with him if he didn't.

We raised our glasses in a silent toast and went to work. To edit together was to clean the slate. I opened the folder and presented Willie with the draft. Felt-tipped pen in hand he read the opening paragraph of the flap copy.

> *Always Stand In against the Curve* is a book for those of us lucky enough to have shot baskets under a driveway goal or shagged fly balls in open fields until it grew too dark to see the hoop or the ball against the sky. Morris makes us remember. He writes about sports but also about growing up in America, about listening to a radio broadcast of a Dodgers game in a Mississippi country store, about girls with double names, about the hold the past has on us, about running effortlessly forever.

- 28 -

Why I Wrote *Rommel and the Rebel*

By 1984 despite the success of the books we'd published—*Mississippi Poems, Helen: A Courtship, Good Old Boy, The Ghosts of Rowan Oak, Terrains of the Heart, Nights under a Tin Roof, Legend in Crimson, North Toward Home*—Yoknapatawpha Press was at a crossroads. My obsession for setting competitive prices for books with print runs of 5,000 or fewer was cutting into potential profits. The industry standard for retail price/unit cost was ten to one. In other words, the retail price of a book should be ten times what it costs to produce. Typically, our markup was six to one. Yoknapatawpha Press needed a book that would produce a hundred thousand dollars in gross sales.

My brilliant idea was *Football Powers of the South*, a sports photo album printed in the same run with a calendar book of twelve university football programs. The odds seemed in our favor. I was betting that the 50,000+ loyal alumni of each school would buy a mere thousand calendars and five hundred books featuring their beloved team. The proposed paperback anthology contained twelve chapters with fifty-plus black-and-white sports photos and twelve chapter-break pages printed in the school colors of each university. Since it was not cost-effective to print one color picture in each signature, my solution was to reprint the calendars on text paper in an overrun of five hundred each, then fold and gather the separate signatures into books. In trimming off the calendar section below the photos we'd be paying for roughly twice the paper of each printed book, but it was cheaper than paying press time to print the photo albums separately.

Dean could have vetoed the project, but true to Maud's example she chose not to complain. The bank loan for $60,000 required both our signatures. The interest rate then was 14 percent. I optimistically thought we'd pay off the loan in six months. All we had to do was get the calendars into the stores.

Between September and Christmas we sold perhaps one-third of what we'd printed. Of course, the calendars came off bookstore shelves in January. I scrambled to remainder a few thousand calendars to shops in twelve university towns for $1 apiece.

Furious at me for squandering our modest capital, Dean declared a time-out. She would spend Christmas with Diane and Michael, who were living in Vermont. I was to stay at home, take care of the dogs, and spend the holiday with Wese and her sister Clara Mae.

Willie, who was planning to drive to Bridgehampton for the holidays, offered Dean and Paige a ride. From Long Island they would rent a car and drive to Vermont. I was tasked with taking Jaybird to his first prom and putting him on a plane to Burlington. Before I knew it, Dean and Paige were heading north in Willie's second-hand Buick, which we'd bought him when his mother's 1971 Plymouth died.

I rented a tuxedo for 'Bird and delivered him to Batesville, Mississippi, where the prom was being held. The next day I packed his suitcase, drove to Batesville where he'd spent the night, and took him to Memphis Airport.

On the way home I remembered that Louise had asked me to get a Christmas tree. I pulled over at Sardis Reservoir. Cutting down a tiny pine sapling with my pen knife was a first, but so, too, was the doomed *Football Powers of the South*.

Clara Mae and I decorated the Charlie Brown tree with three ornaments. We fixed Bloody Marys, exchanged gifts, and watched a Christmas program on TV. This was the only Christmas I would ever spend with Dean's mother and aunt, and looking back I realize how special it was. At the time, however, I was going through the motions. I'd put our independent press in harm's way, my wife had gone north toward home, and I had no one to blame but myself.

Christmas Day was quiet. Just me and the dogs. Flipping through the *Clarion-Ledger* I noticed an article about a Civil War Roundtable lecture in Jackson. A retired army officer named Jack Maxey recalled hosting five German military officers in the 1930s. They'd come to Mississippi to study the Battle of Brice's Crossroads, where Confederate general Nathan Bedford Forrest defeated a Union force that outnumbered his cavalry three to one. Maxey, then a second lieutenant just out of Mississippi State ROTC, claimed that Field Marshal Erwin Rommel was one of the German visitors. I was intrigued.

Over the holidays I forgot about Maxey's story. Then shortly after Dean returned from Vermont the story rose from my subconscious. This was a novel begging to be written: Erwin Rommel tours Brice's Crossroads battlefield, studies Forrest's double-envelopment, then springs the same tactics on the British at Benghazi in 1942.

A businessman would seek additional partners to save a sinking company. My solution was to conceive, write, and sell a novel. But first, I had to contact Maxey. By then I'd lost the clipping about the Roundtable lecture and couldn't remember his name. I went to the Ole Miss library only to learn that their issue of the *Clarion-Ledger* had gotten wet and was ruined. This temporary setback only made me more determined. Straightaway I drove to Starkville and plowed through the MSU library's newspapers until I found the Christmas issue.

I arranged to meet Jack Maxey at Shoney's Restaurant in North Jackson. The taped interview was barely audible. One can hear glasses and dishes clanking in the background, customers talking, waitresses calling in orders. Maxey's story, I saw at once, formed the core of the novel lodged in my subconscious. His ROTC instructor at Mississippi State, he said, was a Nathan Bedford Forrest fanatic who preferred the Civil War to modern military tactics and procedures and took his cadets to the Brice's Crossroads battlefield. As a fictional character he was pure gold, and so was Maxey. His primary duty in the Mississippi army reserves (this was before the national guard) had included feeding and housing CCC workers during the Depression.

"I fed 'em for thirty cents a day," Maxey proudly declared, "and fed 'em good!"

I left Shoney's with a novel in my pocket.

It didn't matter whether Rommel was really among the five Germans who visited Mississippi. In a novel I could even let my fictitious Rommel meet an equally fictitious William Faulkner. As soon as I got home I asked Dean's permission to cast her uncle as a fictional character. By then she had forgiven me for publishing *Football Powers of the South*. She shook her head as if to say, "Some people never change!" and gave me her blessing.

I remembered a Shelby Foote story about going to Shiloh with Faulkner. In the fall of 1981, Foote invited Willie, David Rae, David Sansing, and me to meet him at Shiloh National Park, where he treated us to an unforgettable tour of the battlefield.

Standing in the peach orchard at Shiloh, Foote recalled that as a young man in the early 1950s, on his way to Shiloh from Greenville he stopped at Rowan Oak to see Faulkner. He introduced himself saying, "Mr. Faulkner, my name is Shelby Foote. I am a writer from Greenville. I'm on my way to Shiloh. I was wondering if you would like to go."

"Let me get my hat," Faulkner replied.

On the way they stopped in Corinth, Mississippi, just south of the Tennessee border. Faulkner wanted to buy some bootleg whiskey. At the time, Mississippi was a dry state. Faulkner directed Foote to a mortuary located next door to a church.

"Mr. Faulkner," Foote said, "this is a funeral home and a parsonage. Are you sure this is the right place?" Faulkner told him to wait and see. Foote watched the author knock, pass money through the opened door, and in return receive a pint of whiskey. Faulkner returned to the car.

"Let's go!" he said.

I asked Foote if he learned anything new about Shiloh from Faulkner.

"Mr. Faulkner didn't know all the particulars," Foote replied, "but he had a poet's understanding of the human sacrifice and tragedy."

We were being treated to two magnificent tours: the present one and Foote's tour with Faulkner. Shelby took us, as he had taken Faulkner, to an Indian mound overlooking the Tennessee River. The Indian mound which was slowly caving into the river was marked off limits. Foote knew a secret path. We pushed through thickets and brambles following the same path he'd used before. Reaching the cliff's edge we saw what Forrest (and Foote and Faulkner) had seen: the mighty Tennessee River, sunlight sparkling on its surface, kingfishers diving into a school of minnows.

It was from this mound that Bedford Forrest spotted the Army of the Ohio unloading men and arms from flatboats. Forrest hurried from one senior officer to the next seeking orders to counterattack during the night. None would take responsibility. The next day the Union army turned the tide and forced the Confederates to retreat. Staring down at the shining river I couldn't help imagining Rommel and Faulkner passing the bootleg bourbon back and forth, Rommel interested mainly in historical facts, Faulkner commenting on the Lost Cause of the Confederacy.

"Is this mound where your tour with Faulkner ended?" I asked Foote.

"No," Shelby replied with a grin, "it ended when the whiskey ran out."

I began writing *Rommel and the Rebel* at about the same time Willie Morris was finishing *The Courting of Marcus Dupree*. We'd meet at the kitchen table. One night he'd read a chapter. The next I would read one from my novel in progress.

Willie was especially taken with a chapter in which Speigner and Rommel rent a mechanic's motorcycle. They ride the terrain where the Battle of Brice's Crossroads took place, traveling back in time, crossing, as it were, invisible battle lines between Union and Confederate forces. The two characters can almost hear musket balls flying overhead.

The next morning I found a note in the mailbox which Willie must have deposited at dawn.

> *Boss, I think you've really got something there. Here's to a best seller in the Yoknapatawpha family. Best of luck! Willie.*

Considering the financial hole I'd dug, a novel about Rommel and Faulkner might not save Yoknapatawpha Press, but a decent advance might allow us some breathing room. This proved true six months later when Doubleday bought the novel based on one hundred pages and synopsis.

- 29 -

I Led Two Lives

What had happened to Dean was happening to me. Part of me, the most natural part, was being swallowed by the Faulkner mystique. There were even times when acquaintances unintentionally called me "Dean." Having lived all her life with this identity problem she struggled against being typecast, but for me it was new and unexpected territory.

As I approached fifty I began searching for the Larry Wells that I'd been, the graduate student whom Dean told Sandra Baker she wanted to spend the rest of her life with—former college English instructor, writer, indie press editor and publisher, bass player, and obsessive compulsive who had published two novels, scripted an Emmy-winning documentary, and optioned four screenplays in LA and New York while editing and publishing other writers.

A university administrator in Covington, Kentucky, wrote me praising my second novel, *Let the Band Play Dixie* (which was partly set in Kentucky), saying that he hoped my work at Yoknapatawpha Press would not hinder me from writing fiction. Those words came to haunt me.

At a book convention in New Orleans I found myself at a crossroads. Would I follow the path of editor or writer? Continue as a small press publisher or jump into writing fulltime? In the eyes of the public could I be both?

The Yoknapatawpha Press book exhibit was a short stroll from the Doubleday booth. I decided to pay the sales reps a call. On the way across the convention floor as I morphed from indie publisher to author, I couldn't help noticing that many conventioneers wore disguises. Costumed rabbits, gangsters, and Supermen stalked the aisles. I overheard a snatch of conversation: ". . . *and I came to the realization that there are more important things in life. I can't fight the commercialization anymore.*"

Commercial success, or the lack of it, was fueling my identity crisis. Doubleday's first printing of *Rommel and the Rebel* had sold out in six weeks, yet my editor inexplicably had decided not to issue a second edition. Booksellers and libraries had placed several thousand orders that were unfilled. Wasn't selling books the point of publishing?

There was a reason my book hadn't been reprinted.

Major publishers given the opportunity will interview first novelists and test their promotional skills. Before my novel was published I happened to be visiting New York. I volunteered to give a test interview only to learn that the staff was shorthanded and that an intern would tape the conversation. The young assistant, bright and eager, took me to a vacant office. Apologizing for not having had a chance to read the novel he turned on the tape recorder.

"So, tell me about your book," he said.

I had planned to discuss how I'd been intrigued by reports that Rommel was one of five German officers who had visited Mississippi's Civil War battlefields, and the uncanny similarity between Rommel's military tactics and those of Nathan Bedford Forrest. Both generals used surprise and knowledge of the terrain to defeat their enemies. They also planned down to the last detail. "Shed sweat, not blood" was their motto. Bringing a fictional Rommel to north Mississippi would allow me to introduce him to a fictional William Faulkner, and Dean had given me the family's blessing.

But did I stick to this script?

On impulse, I assumed the book-buying public would be interested that a small press editor had been forced out from behind his desk, so to speak, and in effect was writing above his editorial weight. Like a fit of nausea the truth rose in my throat. I'd gone fishing with a football calendar and wound up writing *Rommel and the Rebel* to save Yoknapatawpha Press.

"Rommel and Faulkner, opposites attract, eh?" the intern interrupted to get me back on subject. After all, I was there to promote my first novel. "Did you see them hitting it off?"

This logical question almost turned me around. In the novel, Faulkner's character had hoped to see combat as an RAF pilot, but WWI ended before he could complete his flight training. He is jealous of Rommel's war record. The Rommel character, on the other hand, is envious of Faulkner's literary success. His book on military tactics, *Infanterie greift an*, "Infantry Attacks," had been a bestseller in Germany, and he is hoping to further his writing career. Faulkner takes Rommel to Shiloh and explains the lost cause of the Confederacy.

But did I answer the intern's question?

No, I was wedded to my own lost cause, which was how *Rommel and the Rebel* arose from the ashes of a sports calendar. The embarrassment and regret building in me for months overrode any sense of equilibrium much less self-preservation. I should have excused myself from the interview and said, "Let me get a good night's sleep and we'll tape the interview tomorrow."

Small press publishing doesn't require courage so much as blind faith in the future. Every fall season was make-or-break for Yoknapatawpha Press. I was like Don Quixote on crack cocaine jousting at windmills. Dean loved me for charging ahead but despaired over my bullheadedness. Now I was guilty of letting down the woman whose mantra was courage. Out poured my rambling, absolution-seeking tale until, mercifully, the intern shut off the tape recorder.

After this disastrous interview Doubleday couldn't trust me to publicize my work. The marketing director had no choice but to write me off. If I wanted to promote the sale of *Rommel and the Rebel* I would be on my own.

When the novel came out I indeed arranged all book promotions and submitted personal copies to reviewers at newspapers and television and radio stations. At book signings I supplied books I had ordered at author discount. In effect I was selling books out of the trunk of my car.

Then the clouds parted.

Ron Harrist, Associated Press bureau chief in Mississippi, wrote a review of *Rommel and the Rebel* focusing on my use—with the family's blessing—of William Faulkner as a fictional character.

Harrist quoted my mother-in-law Louise, who told me that my characterization of Faulkner was so authentic that she "could almost hear Bill speaking." The AP wire story appeared in dozens of newspapers, and Doubleday's first printing of 8,000 copies sold out in six weeks.

At my request, a clerk at Square Books looked up Ingram's sales report, which showed 3,000 copies of *Rommel* on order. I phoned my editor to report continuing demand and to find out if a second printing was in the works.

"We have decided not to reprint the hardcover," she said. "You'll have to wait for the Bantam paperback."

"But . . . the Bantam edition is a year away!" I stammered. "If supply continues, demand could double or triple."

My words fell on deaf ears. It didn't matter that stores were begging for the hardcover edition. I thought of the final scene in *2001: A Space Odyssey* where actor Keir Dullea has been cut loose by the computerized "Al" and is cartwheeling through space.

At the Doubleday booth, the sales reps avoided eye contact. No doubt they'd heard about my author interview. I wouldn't have been surprised if my tape was required listening for interns on "How not to conduct an interview."

I edged over to a cheerful sales representative; and although my first impulse was to shout *When will you reprint my novel?* I asked, instead, who handled reprint decisions.

"It's done by committee," he replied. Then he noticed my novel on the display table. "Oh, I see, you wrote this one. Of course, you have a right to be concerned about your title being out of print this early in the season, but before a second run can be considered we have to evaluate returns. The industry average is thirty percent, you know."

I doggedly repeated that Ingram Books had back orders for 3,000 copies of *Rommel and the Rebel*, which could represent a second wave of sales. Wasn't the book business about getting buzz and riding the wave?

"Sometimes." The rep shrugged. "But in this case we had to wait and see if demand was dropping off." Before he turned away I blurted an offer to pay to reprint 5,000 copies for Doubleday. He frowned. "What do you think we are," he said, "a subsidy press?"

Returning to the small press exhibition area, depression dogging my heels, I was confronted by a self-published author whose children's book I'd agreed to distribute. Sales were not going well.

"Are you running low on copies?" she said hopefully. "I can get some more printed in three weeks. Don't you think sales will pick up at Christmas?"

"Returns are running unexpectedly high," I heard myself saying. "The industry average is thirty percent, you know. We'd better wait and see." Recognizing a chain book-buyer passing by I introduced him to the author. She automatically went into promotion-mode. I rearranged my display so that her children's book was prominently featured.

I'd just turned away when a woman holding a folder approached me. I knew the hungry look. She was bringing me a manuscript for publication.

"Would you be interested in a different kind of children's book?" she said, handing me the folder. Inside was a mockup of a picture book containing cellophane panels, each of which contained photos identified as *Daddy, Mommy, Sister, Granddaddy, Miss Kitty, Fido*. "The trouble with books today," she said confidently, "is that they have too many words."

In 1991 as my fiftieth birthday approached, Willie reached out—with that great Mississippi heart of his, aware that the big five-o is a crossroads for everyone but especially struggling middle-aged writers—and invited me to dinner. Dean and I drove to Jackson to celebrate my birthday, which happened to coincide with Willie and JoAnne's first wedding anniversary and David Rae's receiving a master's degree at the University of Minnesota. At Hal and Mal's Willie presented me with a birthday menu—more poem than menu—which had the intended effect of reminding me of where I came from and, ultimately, who I was and would always be. The titles of the menu items were a song of Mississippi and my native Alabama and a tribute to everyone at the table. The "Waiters" and one of the "Waitresses" he listed on my birthday card were characters from *Good Old Boy*. "Taco Chips Tyrone Ashley" was a shout-out to an Ole Miss running back.

This was Willie at his whimsical best, putting my midlife crisis into perspective. "Happy Birthday, Boss!" he'd written. "Happy Anniversary, JoAnne! Happy Master's Degree, David Rae!"

Table d'hote
Hot Tamales Ozark *Grapes Grenada*
(I love you, Boss, Happy 50th! Miss your daddy too.)
Guacamole Indianola *Bananas Belzoni*
Cheese Straws Yazoo
Cheddar Fromage South Lamar
Pistachios Pocahontas
Smoked Turkey Tallahatchee
Anniversary Cake Kosciusko
Wheat Crackers Tupelo
Taco Chips Tyrone Ashley
Nuts Whitfield
Watermelon Water Valley

Waiters	Waitresses
Spit McGee	Rivers Applewhite
Henjie Henick	Vanna White

Happy Birthday, Boss!
Happy Anniversary, JoAnne!
Happy Master's Degree, Dave Rae!

Chez Four-oh-Eight
September 14, 1991

Table d'hote

Grapes Grenada
Bananas Belzoni

Hot Tamales Ozark
Guacamole Indianola
Golden Gopher
Popcorn
Cheese Straws Yazoo
Cheese Fromage South Lamar
Cheddar Pocahontas
Pistachios Tallahatchie
Smoked Turkey
Cake Kosciusko
Anniversary

I love you, Boss, Happy 50th! Miss you daddy too.

Wheat Crackers Tupelo
Taco Chips Tyrone Ashley
Nuts Whitfield
Watermelon Water Valley

Vin Rouge '88
Vin Blanc '89
Vodka Smirnoff '89
Budweiser '90
Beer Bland '90
Coca-Cola '91
Apple Juice '91
Orange Juice '34

Ice Water Isola
Tea Lemon Zinger

Waitresses
Rivers Applewhite
Vanna White

Waiters
Spit McGee
Henjie Henick

Go, Rebels!!
Go, Tide!!

Wait till next year!
Love + Happy Birthday
JoAnne

- 30 -

Oxford, Too, Was Changing

In 1992, three decades after Faulkner's death, Oxford looked pretty much as it did in his day—modest homes on spacious, tree-shaded lots. But as Faulkner's generation died out, the heirs began selling off family property. Developers from Memphis, Atlanta, and Chattanooga invested in residential lots. The alderperson for our district, Janice Antonow, a farsighted public servant, persuaded/shamed the town council into enacting historic zoning ordinances. It took her several years to convince the council to preserve the square and historic districts surrounding it. The city council was divided on the issue. Mayor John Leslie's vote broke the tie. For a while real estate development was controlled by zoning regulations. Dean and I were grateful to the council members who voted to protect the town's historic neighborhoods.

After Leslie retired, Patricia Lamar ran for mayor. Campaigning door to door she came seeking our support. We asked only that she preserve the historical zoning ordinance, which she agreed to do, shaking hands on her pledge and assuring us that she considered historic zoning "a necessary safeguard." Once elected, however, Lamar went back on her word. Taking half of the council members by surprise and without public discussion the new mayor and her allies on the board voted to revoke Antonow and Leslie's historic zoning ordinance.

Within months most of the saleable property between the square and the campus was snapped up. Proximity to Rowan Oak became prime real estate. The maxim *location, location, location* was never more relevant or ironic. Developments were named for Faulkner novels or characters. A section of Bailey's Woods was renamed "Faulkner's Woods." Overnight, it seemed, eight modern townhouses with basement parking replaced single residences on spacious lots. It was the same all over town.

Oxford welcomed newcomers, but all-out, profit-driven development placed the town's architectural unity at risk. Since many retirees wanted to live close to the campus, traditional neighborhoods between the town and the university were gutted. Real estate values shot up and property taxes doubled. The subtext to the "Walk to the Stadium" advertising slogan was that Oxford was a fountain of youth for Ole Miss alumni.

Despite his reverence for the past, Faulkner had doubts about trying to relive one's youth, writing in *The Mansion*: "Why yes he thought it aint a place a man wants to go back to; the place dont even need to be there no more. What aches a man to go back to is what he remembers."

The new Oxford in fact was nothing like Faulkner's. In his day half the population—black, white, and brown—were related by blood. Black and white neighborhoods intermeshed. When integration arrived in Oxford, common ground was right around the corner.

Faulkner's Oxford, of course, had the advantage of the author's presence. Friends and strangers sought him out. They didn't care if, being lost in thought, the resident laureate failed to say good morning. It was enough to have passed Faulkner on the street.

Oxford attorney Phil Stone, generally accepted as a prototype for Faulkner's fictional lawyers, "Horace Benbow" and "Gavin Stevens," once said, "There'll be people coming to Oxford on account of Bill who would never have heard of the place except for Bill and what he writes."

Stone's prediction led Dean to observe, "I'm glad Phil Stone never knew how right he was. He would not believe the changes Oxford has suffered due in part to Pappy's fame: We were 'discovered' just before the turn of the twenty-first, when several national publications listed Oxford as one of the top 100 small towns to retire in—(or just die in)—rising to the top fifty, and finally the top ten. Oxford was deemed the epitome of traditional southern charm, with swings on porches, hundred-year-old oak trees lining streets, picket fences, flowerbeds in every front yard, and its own literary icon. The developers discovered Pappy was saleable—though I doubt if one in ten of second-home Oxonians have read him or intend to."

Real estate development in Oxford couldn't (and shouldn't) be stopped, but residents hoping for reasonable development expected the city council to keep it under control. "Build dikes with zoning ordinances!" became our motto. But in the end what Oxford needed was a change in leadership.

Along with attorneys Tom and Joyce Freeland, longtime friends Al and Becky Morton, and other like-minded souls, Dean and I cofounded a nonprofit organization called "Citizens for Responsible Development." Our goal was to make people aware of what was happening and to build a coalition to save traditional neighborhoods. When it became clear that the incumbent mayor supported development for its own sake, CRD's emphasis shifted to electing a new mayor. Richard Howorth had been planning to run for alderman at large until Dean told him, "If you don't run for mayor I'll never speak to you again." Howorth admitted that when he went to register as a candidate for office he compulsively marked "mayor" instead of alderman.

When incumbent mayor Lamar refused to debate Richard, we encouraged him to go on cable television in her absence. He received twice the air time, and his television appearance aired on cable every night for a week, giving hundreds of voters a chance to get to know him.

Just before election day we heard a rumor that each of the four hundred registered African American voters had received $100 to influence their vote. I'm not suggesting where the alleged $40,000 payout might have come from, but it wasn't from the Howorth campaign.

On election day poll watchers reported that few African American voters were coming to the polling stations. This low turnout boded ill for the Howorth campaign. By mid-afternoon, Dean and I appealed to Vanessa Jones, granddaughter of our longtime housekeeper, Pearline Jones, to help get out the black vote. Vanessa and her friend Greta Young, Ole Miss coeds well known in Oxford, spent the next three hours taking African American voters to the polls. In Vanessa's words, here is how they pulled it off:

> *Greta and I started out attempting to convince people to vote by talking civic duty to them. What we got back was that the voters didn't know either of the candidates personally, so no, they wouldn't be voting. So, secondly, we applied the "change" agenda that was in the air nationally at the time. This peaked greater interest. But then we started to hear about lack of transportation, having to prepare supper during that time, and a host of other things that would rarely be an issue for people of greater means.*
>
> *There were those who were going to vote anyway—lower and upper class—who said, "Oh, I forgot about that" and would head to the polls. They needed no other incentive than a simple reminder.*
>
> *For others who lacked transportation or had food prep duties, we provided a ride to the polls and took care of kids while their moms went to vote.*
>
> *In just the two-mile radius of C. B. Webb, the low-income apartments, and the Freedman Town subdivision where African Americans initially settled post-Civil War and where some upper middle-class blacks still lived, we found enough folks to rock the vote that day.*

Rock the vote is right. Tom Freeland, Jody Jaeger, and I counted 100 African American voters getting out of these two coeds' cars. Thanks in large part to Vanessa and Greta's efforts, the final count in the mayor's race was Howorth 2,600, Lamar 2,500.

"Pappy and Pearline would have loved it!" Dean declared.

As mayor, Howorth couldn't undo the destruction of traditional neighborhoods, but he managed to redirect and control development and, in so doing, restore sanity and moral compass to the town's administration. One of his first actions as mayor was to organize a historic preservation committee. For the next eight years Richard Howorth worked to preserve Oxford's historical districts; and by the end of his second term, in March 2000 , the town council passed a zoning ordinance supporting historic preservation.

- 31 -

Ghosting with Gertrude

Robert Khayat, vice chancellor at the University of Mississippi, was looking for a ghostwriter. The job: to coauthor a book for philanthropist Gertrude C. Ford, about Edward de Vere, 16th Earl of Oxford (1550–1604). Mrs. Ford was convinced that Edward de Vere was the author of the plays and poems of William Shakespeare. Personable and far-sighted, Khayat had a reputation for getting what he wanted. I found myself being caught up in the sly logic of his scheme.

"Nobody can say for sure if the Earl of Oxford was Shakespeare," he shrugged, stating the obvious. "It's only theoretical. But what if the book was a novel? Write anything you like as long as it's plausible."

Actually, I'd been there and done that. In my first novel I alleged that Rommel came to Mississippi and met William Faulkner. In the second I made up a Blue-Gray bowl game between North and South played at Gettysburg in 1896. Now I was being tasked with speculating that someone other than Shakespeare was Shakespeare. The pay was attractive but for an English major the assignment would take some getting used to.

Keeping Yoknapatawpha Press solvent continued to be a struggle. And by 1987, I was paying college tuition. I took the job.

English professors on both sides of the Atlantic staunchly defend Shakespeare of Stratford-Upon-Avon as the one and only Bard, dismissing adherents of "a second Shakespeare" as lunatic fringe.

What made me accept Khayat's offer was an offhand remark by my favorite professor at Ole Miss, Dr. James Savage. A renaissance scholar from the University of Chicago, Savage once remarked to students in his Ben Jonson seminar, "If any of you happens to be interested in Shakespeare authorship, you would do well to find out all you can about Edward de Vere."

When I went to Jackson to meet Mrs. Ford she greeted me wearing a nightgown. I thought, "Well, she's eighty years old. Maybe she wears a nightgown all the time." As a rite of initiation she gave me a house tour that included a walk-in closet filled with mink coats of every color and jewelry. She hefted a felt bag containing dozens of large diamonds.

"Want to hold it?" she said.

We hadn't known each other five minutes and she was showing off her jewelry. Then a thought occurred to me. Was the walk-in jewelry closet a Mississippi version of the British crown jewels? Khayat had mentioned in passing that Mrs. Ford had a fixation on Queen Elizabeth. My task was to keep an open mind and learn all I could about Edward de Vere and his alleged affair with Queen Elizabeth. But first I had to get along with my patron.

She took me through a hallway with portraits revealing that she was the beautiful and pampered daughter of a US senator from Georgia. And within fifteen minutes she also revealed her motive for hiring me to ghostwrite the novel. By this time we had come to the kitchen where she paused to fix a fresh highball. The leading Earl of Oxford scholars, she said, had refused to admit her into the inner circle.

"We're gonna send those prima donnas to hell!" she added, eyes flashing.

A ghostwriter is at various times collaborator, editor, confidante, psychologist, and psychic. Add boy toy to the list. Mrs. Ford was obsessed not only with proving that Edward de Vere was Shakespeare but was convinced that she, Gertrude, was Queen Elizabeth the First, reincarnated. And she cast me as Edward de Vere, Queen Elizabeth's lover.

Four months later, after exhaustive research into the lives of Edward de Vere and William Shakespeare of Stratford-Upon-Avon, I presented Mrs. Ford with a rough draft of chapter 1. She ordered me to read the chapter to her *in bed.* From then on, the bedroom became her preferred meeting place, and over the following two years I read two full drafts of the novel, chapter by chapter, to her while seated in a bedside chair—my alternative to reclining. More often than not she rejected what I'd written and ordered me to start over.

Mrs. Ford believed with all her heart that "Shake-speare" was the pseudonym of Edward de Vere and that Shakespeare's dramas contained an understanding of court life, politics, and European geography too intricate to have come from an untraveled, self-educated glover's son. What she didn't say, but which I knew all too well, was that de Vere had died in 1604 before some of the revised plays were performed, and that Ben Jonson's preface to the First Folio edition of the plays, published in 1616, paid tribute to William Shakespeare of Stratford as the "sweet swan of Avon."

Speculative fiction relies on factual basis or readers won't believe the story. I attempted to adhere to biographical fact even as Mrs. Ford urged me to push the story into a gray area of supposition. From our conversations, I learned that she'd fired two writers before me. This did not inspire confidence.

My stipend included travel funds. In 1987 Dean and I spent six weeks touring Britain, visiting sites associated with Edward de Vere, and the "Oxfordian movement" as it was called. While in England I submitted chapters by mail to Mrs. Ford, who'd been adamantly opposed to my "leaving her." After I returned to Mississippi our literary tug of war resumed in her pink boudoir. In 1989, I presented her with the finished novel which I had written, I must say, with one arm tied behind me.

Mrs. Ford was not happy with the completed manuscript, which I titled "Shakespeare's Child." (Her preferred title was "Shakespeare's Royal Bastard.") Although the novel remained unpublished she generously bequeathed the income from her $33 million estate to the University of Mississippi. Shortly after her death, construction began on the Ford Center for the Performing Arts.

Another consulting job came along in 1993. A. J. (Jody) Jaeger, director of Mississippi Educational Television, had recently filmed a paddleboat voyage on the Mississippi coordinated by Bill Ferris, founding director of the Center for the Study of Southern Culture at Ole Miss. The three-day cruise on the *Delta Queen* from Memphis to New Orleans showcased southern literature, Civil War history, blues, rock and roll, Cajun music, and jazz. Three hundred passengers signed up for lectures and performances by Alex Haley, Shelby Foote, B. B. King, and Mose Allison.

Jaeger and I met at Smitty's Café in Oxford. Over coffee he told me about the *Delta Queen* project. "If you were going to write the script," he said, "how would you do it?" I was confused. Was I being auditioned as scriptwriter after the fact? He didn't mention that he'd finished filming the river cruise and used up the project's $68,000 budget (donated by the Entergy Corporation) or that ETV lacked content for a projected hour-long program.

"How would you tell the story?" he prompted.

A script would have built-in chronology: the *Delta Queen* paddling through history. I scribbled an outline on a napkin. The cruise began in Memphis with blues and rock 'n' roll featuring B. B. King and Elvis; it moved downriver to the *King Biscuit Hour* radio blues show in Helena, Arkansas; then to Vicksburg and Natchez, where Shelby Foote held forth on the Battle of Vicksburg and how Natchez surrendered to spare its antebellum mansions; then south to Baton Rouge and zydeco and Cajun music; and finally to New Orleans and Mose Allison's jazz performance.

Jody liked my rough outline. He took me outside Smitty's and opened the trunk of his car, which contained fifty-three videocassettes.

"Will you review the cassettes and see what can be done?" he asked. In my surprise, I forgot to ask how much the job paid.

After three weeks of viewing and transcribing videotapes I had logged twenty-two usable minutes of Foote, King, Haley, and Allison entertaining *Delta Queen* passengers. Alex Haley discussed the southern tradition of storytelling and how *Roots* came from his family elders telling stories. B. B. King played the kind of blues that stays with you long after the music stops. Shelby Foote gave a tour of the Battle of Vicksburg during the Civil War and lectured on the antebellum history of Natchez. Mose Allison demonstrated how jazz is an art form that is simultaneously conceived and performed.

The rest of the footage mostly showed people getting on and off the boat holding umbrellas. It rained for two days of the three-day voyage. I asked if I could start from scratch.

"Yes, *play God!*" Jaeger commanded.

Having written a previous script for Mississippi Educational Television, I knew about existing archival footage of Eudora Welty, Governor William Winter, Betty Carter, and historians Eli Evans and Lewis Lord. Jaeger also had footage of Bill Ferriss addressing the overlapping traditions of blues, rock and roll, Cajun and zydeco, Dixieland and jazz. "Return to the River" began to grow of its own accord.

I researched passages about the Mississippi River by Mark Twain, Eudora Welty, and Hodding Carter II. Bob Pickett, ETV's head of production and director of *Return to the River*, arranged for actor James Earl Jones to record the narration and recruited readers to present the historical quotations. Pickett persuaded me to record a Mark Twain quotation from *Life on the Mississippi*. Having no idea what Twain's voice sounded like, I taped my impersonation of Faulkner imitating Mark Twain.

Pickett worked tirelessly to obtain background footage for my script. He rose before dawn to record morning sounds of frogs and birds. He filmed a lightning storm in the Delta and collected archival footage of the Mississippi River between Memphis and New Orleans. His concluding shot was the bow of a ship cleaving the river's surface as Hodding Carter III narrated his father's tribute to the mighty Mississippi: "I believe only that Eden is still attainable, though not easily, that the Mississippi, great sewer, father of waters, master and slave of its self-created earth is destined to become the true artery of a nation's impregnable heart."

Alex Haley died before the documentary aired. The film is dedicated to him. Broadcast simultaneously in Mississippi, Tennessee, Arkansas, and Louisiana, the hour-long documentary *Return to the River* was awarded a 1994 Emmy for Best Regional Production.

- 32 -

World Premiere of *Good Old Boy*

In 1989 Oxford was buzzing over the "world premiere" of the TV movie of *Good Old Boy*. Before Disney Channel aired the film, producer Tom Robertson agreed to a private screening at the Hoka Theatre. Willie's fans planned an elaborate celebration.

The book-to-movie adaptation began when Robertson, of Multi-Media Associates in New York City, read a 1987 *Ladies Home Journal* story excerpted from Dean's book, *The Ghosts of Rowan Oak*. Robertson phoned our press to inquire about other children's books. I told him about *Good Old Boy*. Having grown up in Arkansas, Robertson knew the Mississippi Delta and was familiar with Morris's work. I sent him a review copy, and he subsequently purchased film rights.

Disney Channel would acquire broadcasting rights from Multi-Media and over the next two years aired *Good Old Boy*, aka *The River Pirates*, a reported eighty-eight times.

But first came Oxford's world premiere of *Good Old Boy, the Movie*. The party started at Syd and Harry's (now City Grocery). Decked out in a tuxedo with a rose in his lapel Morris was being interviewed by Ole Miss Communications when Hannah showed up in suit, tie, and aviator glasses. It was the only time I saw him wear a suit. Vernon Richards's video camera captured the moment that Hannah took over the interview.

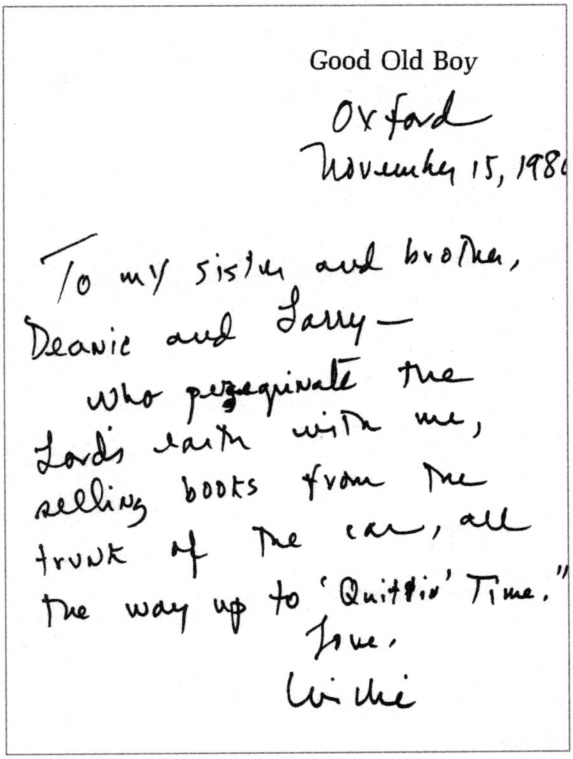
Good Old Boy

Oxford
November 15, 198

To my sister and brother,
Deanie and Larry—
who peregrinate the
Lord's earth with me,
selling books from the
trunk of the car, all
the way up to 'Quittin' Time."
Love,
Willie

Barry: Mr. Morris, will you tell us a little about this production tonight?

Willie: Well, Mr. Hannah, I would put it on a level with "Gone with the Wind," but it doesn't have my name on it. It says Walt Disney. But I think it's a good movie. As you know we're donating the proceeds of tonight's showing at the Hoka to Mr. Hannah's favorite charity, the Humane Society. He and I love dogs and cats, and maybe even armadillos.

Barry: Here's to armadillos and old Pete and to all of us.

Willie: And all of us!

More than a hundred of Willie's fans were on hand when my stepson Jon drove him into the Hoka parking lot. The convertible top was down, and Jon's dog Denver perched in his lap, paws on the steering wheel, recreating the scene in *Good Old Boy* when Willie's dog Skip "drives" a roadster. When Ron Shapiro's klieg lights found Morris, the roar of applause could be heard at the courthouse.

Where else could this have happened except at the Hoka—Ronzo's legendary coffeehouse/cinema where we hung out with friends, drank cinnamon coffee laced with bourbon, and enjoyed watching movies that we'd already seen.

Shapiro welcomed the celebrants to the Hoka. "Before we show the film," he said, "the Chadwicks have a song for Willie."

Ole Miss tennis coach Billy Chadwick, his twin brother Barney, and Billy's wife, Julie, former lead singer in their high school rock band, performed a song that Dean and I had composed with them a couple of days before the premiere. "The Joker at the Hoka, the Last of the Good Old Boys" began like this.

This song's for Willie, the laureate of Yazoo.
He's got his first movie, with rave reviews, too,
We love you, Willie! you're a bundle of joy-yyyy.
He's the joker at the Hoka, the last of the good old boys.
He went out to Texas from down in Yazoo,
Went to England and to Paris and to New York, too,
'Cause he's a writer—yes, he's a literary man.
He's the joker at the Hoka, and Willie we're your biggest fans . . .

"Now, I've been called a lot of things in my life," Willie responded when it was his turn to address the audience, "but never the joker at the Hoka! Actually I'm rather honored. The Chadwicks are actually appearing next week at Radio City Music Hall in New York City. Or at least the old Dixie Theater in Yazoo City. I'd like to thank my old comrade, Ronzo Shapiro, who's always loyal, and the Hoka Theatre which I think is synonymous with Oxford and the university. Every great university needs a Hoka. It represents so much to Oxford and Ole Miss in terms of continuity and everything else. I want to thank Ron for setting this up tonight and Julie Chadwick for the hors d'oeuvres.

"I'd like to congratulate Barry Hannah, my fellow scribbler, who has just finished his latest book, *Boomerang*. He's a luminary at the Humane Society, and the proceeds from this evening's program are going to the Humane Society. Barry and I both love dogs and cats and sometimes express mutual affection for armadillos—late at night in the Gin.

"I got this tuxedo for $39.95 plus tax and they didn't even throw in socks.

"I want to thank Gerald Turner, chancellor of Ole Miss, for his unequivocal loyalty and support of this writer and of the visiting writers program at the university. Gerald deeply comprehends the literary traditions of Ole Miss and Mississippi. My abiding gratitude also to Porter Fortune for his counsel and sustenance over the years. Thank you, chancellor, and thank you, Chancellor Emeritus.

"To Deanie and Larry at the Yoknapatawpha Press . . . what does one say about Deanie and Larry! Thanks for believing in this book, *Good Old Boy*, which I wrote many years ago. Thanks for all those nights around the kitchen table at Miss Maud Falkner's house, listening on the radio to the Ole Miss games, listening to the chimes of Mr. Bill's courthouse.

"Film director Tom Robertson invited Dean and Larry and me to the wrap party in Natchez, where they were making the movie, to meet the kids in the cast. These Hollywood kids only missed occasionally the southern accent. When we got there it was about 108° which is about as hot as Mississippi gets. I was sitting by myself in the bar at the Sheraton having a lemonade when I felt this tug at my elbow. I looked up and saw this handsome, mischievous-looking, twelve-year-old boy wearing a blue baseball cap and clothes of the World War Two era. He said, 'Are you Willie?' And I said, "Yeah.'

"And he said, 'Willie, where you been? We've been looking for you for three days.'

"I said, 'Well, who are you?'

"And he said, 'I'm Willie!'

"This movie is very autobiographical as was the book. Disney stuck to the spirit of it, I think. Most of the things you see in this movie really happened in 1944. I've seen it, and may I say it was a spooky feeling. It gave me goosebumps. There, all of a sudden, were my parents long dead, my grandparents long dead. My crazy aunt Sue was played by the immortal Maureen O'Sullivan. My old dog Skip, and of course, me. And it brought back to me, in a bizarre rush, a horrendous déjà vu. But in a funny way it gratifies me. I hope you enjoy it, and I want to thank my many friends and all of you here tonight for coming, and this is a great party, and let's whup the Tennessee Volunteers!"

For Morris, the Natchez wrap party was a trip down memory lane. He loved meeting actors whose characters were based on members of his family and boyhood pals such as Henjie and Bubba. For a moment I think Willie wanted to believe that actors Richard Farnsworth and Maureen O'Sullivan *were* his grandfather and aunt. When he saw them, he wept.

We didn't know it then, but Oxford's "world premiere" of *Good Old Boy* brought the community together in a spontaneous celebration of literature and film that foreshadowed today's Yoknapatawpha Arts Council and the Oxford Film Festival.

- 33 -

Louise Hale Faulkner Meadow (1913–1994)

When Dean learned that her mother had Alzheimer's she thought of Gabriel Garcia Marquez's line, "People don't die when they should but when they can."

Dean visited Louise every day at Yalobusha County Hospital in Water Valley. She sat by her mother's bed working crossword puzzles or reading magazines, while Louise talked to herself. She wheeled her mother outside and sat on a bench in the sun. Alzheimer's is contagious. It infects not only the patient but those charged with his or her care. Louise greeted Dean with a cold, fixed gaze, furious at circumstances beyond her control.

In January 1994, a major ice storm settled over north Mississippi just as Louise came home from the hospital. Trees fell on power lines. There was no electricity or water. Streets were frozen over. We couldn't drive to the grocery or have food delivered. With a gas stove lit with matches, we melted snow for drinking water. Dean made a tuna casserole and carried it to her mother's house through ice and guilt a foot deep.

Strapped in a wheelchair Louise stared as if to say *Who are you? What's going on?* Dean opened the casserole cover to indicate what was inside. Louise plunged her fingers into the steaming casserole and flung the noodles in Dean's face. It was just another volley in their twenty-four-year war.

After a week of arm-fighting Louise, the nurses served notice. They couldn't believe a woman that old and frail could be that strong. Dean arranged for Louise to be readmitted to the Yalobusha Hospital and posted want ads for nurses. What memory Louise had remaining was so diminished that when Dean brought her home from hospital she did not recognize her sister Clara Mae.

To celebrate her mother's ninetieth birthday Dean baked a red velvet cake. Louise ate a bite and smiled. For a few precious hours she was the Wese of Dean's youth, ready to laugh and share a memory. Dean's dear, desperate, wretched mother, her best friend and fiercest rival, was saying goodbye.

A week later Louise was diagnosed with pneumonia. Dean was about to call for an ambulance but Clara Mae, speaking both as sister and agoraphobic, said, "Let her meet her Maker at home." Dean replaced the receiver. Her mother had earned the right to die in her own bed.

A practical nurse came to sit with her. At dawn we were awakened by a call from the coroner, whom the nurse had summoned. We arrived to find coroner and funeral home attendants, all fairly large men, squeezed into the compact living room with Clara Mae and the nurse. The coroner told us that heart failure was the cause of death.

Dean couldn't make herself enter the bedroom. For the sake of closure I urged her to say goodbye to her mother. My presumption made her angry.

"It's easy for you to tell me to look at Wese!" she said. "Your parents are still alive. How do you know what I am going through?" Finally, consumed by grief and shame she peeked through the bedroom door. Louise's dead hands were clenched as if she'd fought to the end.

"Don't be fooled by appearances," I said. "She's flying with your father."

Clara Mae kept a bottle under the sink. As the bourbon kicked in Dean remembered Louise's taking her to the ice cream parlor in Clarksdale when she was six. "Wese bought me chocolate ice cream but the real treat was hearing about my father. She'd tell me how she and Dean would play cards in airport hangars waiting for the weather to change. As soon as the sun came out they grabbed leather helmets and goggles and ran to the plane. My father never told her where they were going and she never asked. Wese said, "*It was wonderful, lamb!*"

"I couldn't finish the ice cream," Dean recalled. "I was too busy imagining how the plane's exhaust smelled and feeling the prop wash in my face."

Clara Mae took up the story. For Louise, marrying Jimmy Meadow was like going from plane crash to train wreck. Meadow was a competent newspaperman by day and a drunk by night. His death in 1958 finally allowed Louise to resume a normal life. In the early sixties she had cancer of the uterus and underwent a successful but painful radiation treatment. She recovered and began a platonic relationship with a university professor. One night driving back from Memphis the professor went to sleep at the wheel. The car struck a tree. The professor wasn't hurt, but Louise crashed through the windshield and shattered her collarbone. The impact knocked out her front teeth and broke her cheekbones. To rebuild her face required multiple surgeries. "But we won't dwell on that!" Clara Mae said and put away the family album.

Dean hadn't told me about the radiation treatment or the car wreck. I floundered in the *if-only-I'd-known* syndrome which afflicts those who live in the moment. Dean, however, was at home at a wake. She had never stopped loving, or appreciating, her mother. I on the other hand was wishing that I had paid more attention to Louise. For twenty-three years she and I wasted valuable time skirmishing over nothing. Dean took the long view, and remaining faithful to Miss Maud's philosophy, never complained. I saw at last why she forgave her mother for all the insults and anger. Louise had suffered enough for two lifetimes.

Clara Mae found another family album and showed me how beautiful Louise had been in her youth. Mae, younger by a few years, had been in awe of her only sister. I raised my glass saying,

"To Louise, bless her," and hoped Dean heard the regret in my voice.

One album chronicled the ten years Louise lived in Miss Maud's house before Dean came home. As the pictures indicated, she'd been a charming hostess and kept Miss Maud's home exactly as it had been when Maud died in 1960.

"I wish you had known her then," Dean said.

"I'll settle for the Louise I knew," I said and recalled a Fourth of July when we put out lawn chairs in the front yard to watch distant fireworks.

"Isn't Oxford a beautiful place!" observed Louise.

"It sure is, Weesie," Willie replied tongue in cheek. "Don't you think somebody should write about it?"

"Touché, Willie," Louise laughed.

Clara Mae recalled how Louise kept the family in an uproar. One night Louise, in her cups, decided to end my relationship with Dean by shooting me. Mae phoned Dean saying, "Louise is on a tear!" She'd hidden their father's hunting rifle and locked Louise in her bedroom. Minutes later she phoned back to say Louise had crawled out the window. Dean had phoned me saying "lock your door," then drove to St. Peter's Cemetery and found her mother weeping beside Dean Swift Faulkner's grave.

"Larry was never in no danger," Mae said. "The rifle wasn't loaded."

"Now you tell me!"

"Wese did the best she could," Dean said.

"Hold onto that thought," said Clara Mae, closing the scrapbook.

The funeral home phoned. They needed a family member to approve Louise's appearance for visitation. Dean was in no shape to go. I volunteered.

At the funeral home I was taken to the viewing room. I was relieved to see how composed and peaceful Louise looked. Her hair was tinted blue and waved. Mae had selected burial clothing, a white blouse with lace collar, velvet jacket, and costume jewelry. She looked as if she were resting before a cocktail party.

Less than an hour before, I'd laughed at Mae's description of Louise climbing out the window with murder on her mind. Now, to make peace with myself, and because Dean was counting on me to represent the family, I felt the need to say some words over her with the funeral home attendant as my witness.

I imagined Louise as a young bride flying to air shows with her husband, tossing air show posters on the streets, passing a hat at performances, cheering when the biplane safely landed. And then after losing her husband, joy born of sorrow. On March 22, 1936, her daughter was born. From that day forward the memory of her first marriage could be summed up in one word: *Dean*.

"Her name was Louise Hale Faulkner Meadow," I said, "or MoWese, as she was affectionately known. She was the wife of a pilot and would fly with him anytime, day or night, regardless of crosswinds or low visibility. She never asked where they were going. She had complete faith in him. She wanted only to be by his side. I hope a barnstormer is out there waiting. I'd like to thank Wese for bringing my Dean into the world and for swerving at the last moment and for plugging my novel and babysitting the children. I'm sorry we didn't know each other better."

We buried Louise next to Dean Swift Faulkner. The sun was shining, the sky an unhurried blue. Which clergyman would preside? Louise's denomination was murky. She'd grown up Baptist but switched faiths on any given Sunday. The last church she attended was First Presbyterian of Oxford. Dean asked the Presbyterian minister, Reverend Sam Marshall, to perform the graveside service.

With the aid of valium and bourbon Clara Mae left her sanctuary to attend her sister's funeral. My son Lawrence escorted Dean on his arm. I escorted Mae-Mae. The burial took place in the J. W. T. Falkner plot with its marble obelisk, iron fencing, and scrolled gravestones. Many of Wese's friends and neighbors were present.

As the minister completed the service a small plane flew over the cemetery. The Oxford airport was a mile from the cemetery, the pilot doubtless on final descent. Dean and I exchanged a hopeful glance. Both of us wanted to believe that the plane had come for Louise and that Dean's father was at the controls. We were convinced that the Cessna waggled its wings.

\- 34 -

I Killed Willie

I WASN'T THERE WHEN HANNAH BROKE INTO WILLIE'S HOUSE. Barry himself denied it ever happened. Dean and I pieced together a scenario from eyewitnesses including Willie's and Barry's friends.

In May 1990, Hannah was carousing at the Downtown Grill, a local hangout of sorority girls and middle-aged men. When the bar closed Hannah invited two coeds to—not his own house a block off the square but—16 Faculty Row.

"There's always a party going on at Willie's," he told them. "He'll be glad to see us!"

They didn't trust Barry but being coeds they drove him to Faculty Row. Willie's car was parked in the driveway. The house was dark except for a TV flickering at the bedroom window. What Hannah didn't know was that Willie was in bed with the "flu"—his expression for a hangover. Hannah piled out of the BMW.

"Come on, girls," he said. "Let's surprise ol' Willie."

Smelling a rat, the coeds peeled off. Abandoned and alone Hannah stood in the driveway. His house was less than a mile away, but he was afraid that if he walked home the cops, who never let anybody have any fun, would pick him up. Good ol' Willie wouldn't wish that on his worst enemy.

The kitchen door was locked but the glass pane begged to be broken. Noticing firewood stacked under the landing he helped himself to a piece, smashed the glass, and let himself in. Lying in bed watching TV, Willie heard the crash. All he owned of value were inscribed books; and in Mississippi nobody (except Hannah) stole books. Then he heard someone using his telephone. He recognized the flat, laconic voice.

"I couldn't believe Hannah broke into my house!" he later told us.

Hannah called his motorcycle buddy, Larry DeBord, saying, "I killed Willie!" Before DeBord could ask what happened, Willie jumped out of bed and stormed buck naked into the living room. Taking the smaller Hannah by the scruff of the neck, he dragged him through the kitchen and threw him out. Forget mutual affection for dogs, cats, and armadillos. Barry had gone too far.

On the way back to his bedroom Willie cut his feet on the broken glass.

What happened to these distinguished men of letters? Is there a dark side in writers that counterbalances their nobility of expression? How can they write like angels but live like they are possessed?

Willie never was jealous of Barry or envious of his literary awards. As an essayist and, perhaps more pertinently, an editor, Morris focused on contemporary thought and events outside himself. Barry's power came from within. He inhabited his own imagination and mined it for short stories about love, music, pain, and death. Neither presented a threat to the other, but Barry's competitiveness forced him to bang on other writers' doors and occasionally bash one in. Morris never quite forgave Barry for making casually destructive remarks. And Barry could not forgive Willie for being so damned loveable.

We along with their legion of friends and fans loved them despite, not because, and both brought out the best in us.

Willie washed his bloody feet in the bathtub, limped back to bed, lit a cigarette, and began thinking seriously about moving to Jackson. On the kitchen stoop Barry listened at the broken windowpane, let himself in, opened a fifth of bourbon, and tossed away the cork. Moments later Willie heard a familiar voice making a phone call. Barry had reached out to Glennray Tutor, his friend and illustrator of several of his dust jackets.

"Hello?" Tutor answered sleepily.

"I killed Willie," Barry said.

"Who is this?"

"Me, Barry."

"What do you mean, you killed Willie?"

"He's bleeding like a stuck pig."

"What's the matter with him?"

What, indeed, was the matter with Willie? The trouble with auditioning tall tales in real time is that life itself is in a constant state of revision. Hannah's first rule of writing was to start with a decent sentence, and it was impossible to improve on *I killed Willie*. He couldn't backtrack and explain mundane details: "I broke a window and Willie accidentally cut his feet on the glass." Each sentence had to outdo its predecessor. It was dog-eat-dog in the world of literature.

While Glennray waited for an answer, Larry DeBord arrived and banged on the door.

Barry hung up on Glennray and dialed the home of Evans Harrington, the former English department chairman (who asked me if he could take a chance on Hannah). Outside the living room window Larry DeBord (my co-dedicatee in *The Tennis Handsome*) shined a flashlight through the window. Hannah hung up in Harrington's face and let DeBord in, saying, "What took you?"

Willie heard them trampling broken glass as they left. For him the writing was on the wall. It was time to leave Oxford.

Back at his house, Hannah phoned Glennray in a celebratory mood. "Come over and I'll throw a couple steaks on the grill and—"

Glennray said, "Wait a minute. What about Willie? What's the matter with him?"

Hannah hesitated. What was the matter with Willie? Geez, where did one begin?

"*He's an alcoholic!*"

Truth be told, Barry did not run off his rival single-handedly. The next morning Willie awoke to the thunder of motorcycles. A photographer and two dentists from Nashville had gotten it into their heads to ride to Oxford and surprise ol' Willie. They planned to buy him breakfast at Smitty's.

Willie looked at his watch in disbelief. It was eight a.m. In leather motorcycle jackets, helmets tucked under their arms, the would-be Hells Angels trooped up the kitchen steps. They found the door pane smashed. In the kitchen shards of glass and bloody footprints spoke of a rumble. Things were looking up. They followed the bloody footprints to a bedroom. The photographer tapped on the door. There was no response. He tapped again. The door jerked open and like Zeus in a bloody toga Willie filled the doorway.

"*Get out, get out, get out, get out!*" he bellowed.

Hannah's break-in was symptom, not cause. Everyone wanted a piece of him. There had been too many lonely nights when he brought strangers home from the bar. No wonder people came banging on his door. And Oxford itself had changed. "A hot house for writers," Morris called it. He was leaving a town that had adored him feeling used up and betrayed. Teaching had taken too much of his time and energy, and he still had *Taps* and *New York Days* to finish.

If *The Courting of Marcus Dupree* had been the best seller it could have been he might not have left Oxford; but when Hannah broke into his house the die was cast.

He packed the bare necessities—his Dopp kit, a single starched dress shirt on a hanger, khakis, socks and shorts, a bottle of Scope, carton of Viceroys, school tie and blue blazer—and left 16 Faculty Row making sure to leave the doors wide open.

Dean and I were stunned that Willie had left without saying goodbye. When I heard, I went to check on his house. The doors were indeed open and the air conditioner running. I shut up the house with a sense of resignation. We had invested our resources and emotions in Willie Morris's well-being. His books had made the Yoknapatawpha Press imprint widely known and respected. We'd supported his best interests in every way possible. At the same time we knew that he felt hemmed in by circumstances, that there were books in him waiting to come out.

Writers live for self-expression. If they compromise they are lost. This dedication to one's talent, less an obsession than a calling, appealed to something deep in us and especially to Dean, for whom literature was religion.

Willie had been in Oxford a decade. It was time to let go.

- 35 -

Farewell to Willie

MOVING TO JACKSON PROVED TO BE THE BEST DECISION for Morris. A year later he married JoAnne Prichard, his editor at University Press of Mississippi. He wrote *The Ghosts of Mississippi*, about the second trial of Byron de la Beckwith, and served as a consultant for the movie adaptation. He published *New York Days* and was on the verge of publishing a best-selling children's book, *My Dog, Skip*.

Four years later Willie invited Dean and me to a football game. Alcorn State University was playing Southern University in Lorman, Mississippi. A new chapter in sports history was about to be written. Alcorn quarterback Steve "Air" McNair was poised to break the NCAA's all-time offensive yardage record. Willie begged us to go with him. History was about to be made and the "Stable" needed to be there, he said.

A mile from the Alcorn State campus Mississippi state troopers manned a roadblock. To park on the university campus drivers needed a special permit. Willie was prepared. At a Kinko's in Jackson he'd had a "New York Times press pass" printed. "Show him the press pass, Deanie," he whispered, "and *look like a reporter!*" The trooper, who doubtless had seen every trick in the book, shook his head and waved us through. We parked near the stadium where the public address system boomed Mozart and the smell of barbeque rose from a hundred grills.

In those halcyon days before iPhones good things happened by chance. Like a pointer stalking quail David Rae Morris, a photographer's bag over his shoulder, found us among hundreds of parked cars. He was covering the game for the Associated Press. Sportswriter Rick Cleveland instinctively homed to our tailgate party. Morris had packed a picnic basket with a bucket of Kentucky fried chicken, Cokes, chardonnay, and a 1.5-liter bottle of Smirnoff. We toasted Willie on the publication of his memoir *New York Days*, which Little, Brown had published the previous year. He accepted our congratulations with a smile and a shrug.

A look passed between us. We both remembered the night at the Sizzler when we discussed *New York Days*, a sequel to *North Toward Home*, Willie's autobiography, which opens with the unforgettable line, "I came to the city, and it changed my life."

"Where does the story start?" mused Willie that night at the Sizzler.

Based on recollections he'd shared, I suggested he begin with the day he hit rock bottom. He'd just resigned as editor-in-chief of *Harper's*. His wife, Celia, was considering a divorce. And needing someone to blame Willie became obsessed with Celia's psychiatrist. He staked out the doctor's office and at closing time trailed the psychiatrist through subway changes like Popeye shadowing the Frenchman in *The French Connection*. It was raining when they reached Greenwich Village. Morris followed his intended victim to a townhouse. As the doctor closed his umbrella he looked over his shoulder. Morris stood at the foot of the steps, hatless and seething, raindrops streaming down his cheeks.

"Standing in the rain with nobody to blame but yourself," I prompted. "Flashback to the events that brought you to that moment of despair. Being hired at *Harper's*, learning the trade, late nights at the office. The glory days leading up to the March 1971 issue of *Harper's* when you published Norman Mailer's *The Prisoner of Sex* and *Harper's* sold the most copies in its history. Turning that issue of the magazine into a book was beyond reason, the act of a madman or an angel, unprecedented in the magazine industry. Like when you were student editor of the *Daily Texan*, and the university wouldn't allow you to publish a story critical of the oil industry, and you ran a blank space where the editorial was supposed to go. Cover everything that led to that crisis. The book ends there at the psychiatrist's stoop. Soaking wet. The rage draining from your body. Only then do you accept responsibility for what has happened to you. That's a book anybody would love to read."

"That's it, boss!" Willie said, making notes on napkins.

We write to please ourselves, and that's how it ought to be, but I've always wished that Willie had followed my suggestions. Who knew better than he that any editor worth his salt has the writer's back.

At Jack Spinks Stadium, Alcorn State fans of all ages welcomed us with smiles and handshakes. The temperature was around 95 degrees in full sun. Willie was sweating through his red golfing shirt. Quarterback Steve McNair wearing jersey number 9 led his teammates into the stadium. The Alcorn Braves circled the field at a lope making right angles at the corners, each player spinning as he turned the corner.

Former Alcorn State coach Marino (The Godfather) Casem once observed, "In the Deep South football is religion and Saturday is the holy day." Now the Braves closed ranks in a tight circle, heads bowed, holding their helmets in the air as a minister delivered an invocation.

The pregame ceremony was a prayer in motion. Both university bands played. The rival drum majors tried to outperform each other. A bare-chested Alcorn "Brave" mascot in war bonnet hoisted the Alcorn banner and led players in gold helmets and purple jerseys onto the field. Southern won the toss and chose to kick.

On the first series of downs McNair threw an interception.

"He's tight!" a nearby Alcorn fan yelled.

"Going for too much, too soon," Willie responded, and the fan glanced over his shoulder and touched his cap.

McNair operated a no-huddle, run-and-gun offense. He took the snap in shotgun formation. At home in the pocket, he checked his receivers. Seeing the primary receiver covered, he scrambled and motioned his secondary receivers to go deep. His calm, unhurried throwing motion seemed choreographed. His brother, Tim, Number Seven, caught the pass.

"Go on, Steve, throw it to your brother. Make Mama happy!" yelled the fan in front of us, glancing at Willie for confirmation.

"Yeah, make Mama happy!" Willie echoed. They exchanged a high five. This was the crowd-pleasing Willie at his best. He might as well have been wearing a sign reading "Pied Piper at work."

The Southern University band's trumpet section stood and played a cadenza. The Alcorn cheerleaders performed backflips. And using the clipped style of a play-by-play announcer Willie began to call the game for anyone within earshot.

"Tight end across the middle," he said.

"Hey, Number Nine," Willie's new sidekick echoed, "throw it in the air and run down the field and catch it your own self!"

Our rooting section was taking shape. Writing on the back of a check I began keeping a running total of the yardage McNair needed to break the intercollegiate offensive record. Willie glanced at my notes.

"My computer analyst," he announced, "says McNair has sixty yards and needs two hundred and four to break the record."

"How many yards to go?" the fan said a few minutes later. Other Alcorn boosters were listening.

"Let me check with my computer analyst," replied Willie, checking my latest calculation. "One hundred sixty-four!" he yelled. And, like a common prayer this number was passed from fan to fan. *One hundred sixty-four . . . hundred sixty-four . . . hundred sixty-four.* McNair continued to pile up yardage as if a shroud was being lifted, the Lord fast-forwarding the clouds, my calculations shrinking: 82 . . . 74 . . . 57 . . . 31. With only 6 yards to reach the record we stood blinking in anticipation of being dazzled.

"Ten dollars says this is the play!" sang the indefatigable fan.

Providence seemed to slow the action as McNair faded back for a pass. Seeing his receivers covered, he scrambled around right end. Needing six yards to break the record, he gained twenty-two. The Southern player who tackled him helped him up and shook his hand. Players of both teams lined up to congratulate him. A roar of benediction filled Jack Spinks Stadium.

"God is good! Thank you, God!" cried our fellow fan. Dean and Willie and I exchanged high fives with everyone within reach. The referee called time-out. In both end zones hundreds of gold and purple helium-filled balloons were released.

"Steve McNair," said an announcer over the public address system, "has broken the career yardage record of fifteen thousand and forty-nine yards set by Brigham Young quarterback Ty Detmer." Coach Jones and his staff and players rushed onto the field to congratulate Number Nine.

"Don't forget your mama!" shouted the all-knowing fan. McNair climbed into the stands and gave the game ball to his mother.

Coach Marino Casem was right. Football isn't just a sport. It is a lifetime of shared jubilation. Morris captured that spirit in *Always Stand In against the Curve*, which Dean and I had the honor of publishing. "In the course of human events, as all mystics comprehend," he wrote, "there can be a magic, defying all logic, which will seize a moment, something absurd and indeed existential, undergirded by old unfathomable mysteries—the eternal enigmas of the Old Testament, for instance—and this, of course, is the material of poets."

On the way back to Jackson we stopped at Windsor Ruins, twenty-three Corinthian columns that stand naked under the sky, all that is left of the largest antebellum Greek revival mansion ever built in the state. Windsor Mansion was located on a plantation that covered 2,600 acres. The house was constructed by slaves between 1859 and 1861. Having amassed great wealth, a cotton planter built his mansion four miles from the Mississippi River. This outdoor blues museum was especially relevant after what we'd just witnessed in Lorman.

Here was the Mississippi that Morris understood and which fueled his passion for history. Here were the long shadows of Mississippi's accursed past, and yet that very afternoon an African American athlete had transcended race and injustice to bring distinction to his university and his state. We stood among the historic ruins soaking in the irony.

Willie was a charter member of the Yoknapatawpha Press stable and kitchen cabinet. To echo his inscription in *Faulkner's Mississippi* our friendship and collaboration with Willie was quintessential to our very existence. We'd gone to Lorman to say goodbye but none of us, with the possible exception of Dean, knew how.

When I received a call from a friend on August 1, 1999, saying that Willie had suffered a heart attack and was on life support, I felt a physical sense of loss. Each time someone close to me died I realized, for the first time, what I had most admired about them. I missed my mother's voice, how she sang hymns to herself while she worked, her deep-throated laughter. I missed my father's purposeful touch, always gentle. When Willie died I missed everything.

His quick answers, the depth and breadth of his knowledge, his sense of humor, his capacity for joy and sorrow, his practical jokes, his editor-in-chief's confidence that he could mend any

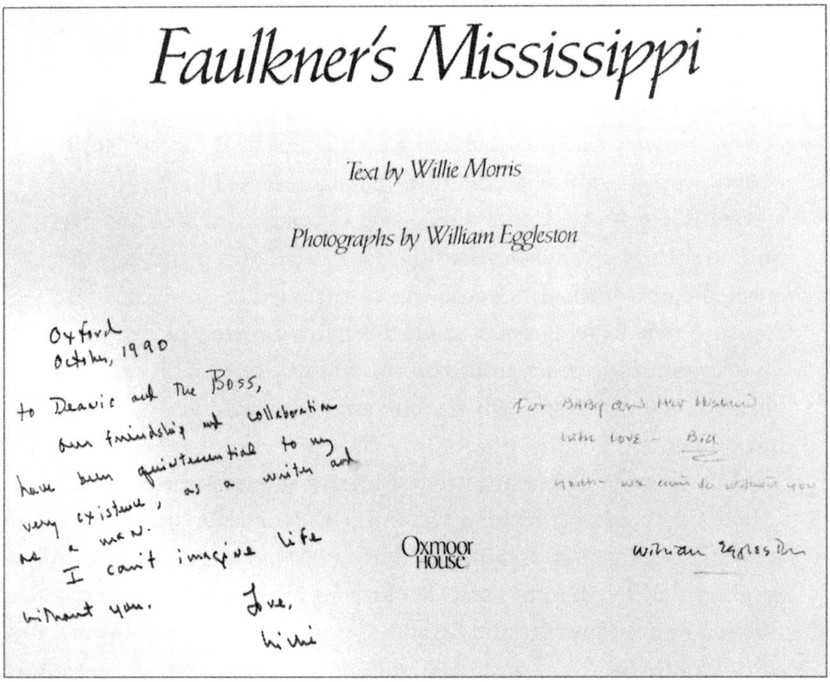

Faulkner's Mississippi

Text by Willie Morris

Photographs by William Eggleston

Oxford
October, 1990
to Deanie and The Boss,
our friendship and collaboration
have been quintessential to my
very existence, as a writer and
as a man.
I can't imagine life
without you.
Love,
Willie

For Baby and Her Husband
with love — Bill

William Eggleston

Oxmoor House

manuscript, add the needed word or phrase. I missed singing WWI songs with him. I missed anonymous phone calls with terrible German or British accents.

I missed his felt-tipped pen.

At Willie's funeral every pew in Yazoo City's First United Methodist Church was filled. His widow, JoAnne, asked Dean to sit with her and David Rae. I was an honorary pallbearer. Will Campbell, noted southern historian, humorist, and ordained minister, led the service. A dozen writers and editors had flown in from the East Coast—the same ones whose names Willie had added to his "speakers" list while planning his funeral in 1981, plus a few he'd left out. I could see him drumming his fingers on the kitchen table.

"Should we include him, Deanie?" Willie had asked.

Will Campbell directed the congregation to stand. Self-conscious and expectant we rose.

"Everybody say Willie!" Campbell commanded.

Willie.

"Like you mean it."

WILLIE!

"Say Amen."

AMEN.

"Please be seated."

It was impossible not to imagine Willie chuckling in the eaves. One summer day when Bill Styron was visiting Oxford, we went for a drive. Willie and David Rae were with us. Willie, who collected cemeteries the way other people collect stamps, surreptitiously dropped a note on a grave. Many of the gravestones bore a laminated photo of the deceased. A scrap of paper fluttered innocently on a grave bearing the image of a white-bearded Jehovah. Willie turned his back and waited for Styron to stumble on it. The note read *Lie down in darkness with me. It aint as bad as you think.*

Styron read it at a glance and turned away. Willie puffed a Viceroy 100 and stared at a passing cloud. We got in the car and drove back to Oxford. Neither of them mentioned the note.

Our phone would never ring at two in the morning. Dean and I would never lie in bed counting the rings, knowing that Willie had put down the receiver to light a cigarette. Never again would Dean mutter, "Wait, see if he hangs up."

Never again would I pick up and answer, "Yoknapatawpha Press, please leave a message at the tone."

Never again would a voice with a fake Yankee accent reply, "For five thousand dollars, what's the capital of Vermont?"

Never again would I nod off during the ensuing monologue and Dean gently take the phone from my hand.

Campbell led the congregation in singing Willie's favorite hymn, "Abide with Me." Dean and I joined mourners walking from the Methodist church to the Yazoo City cemetery, a quarter of a mile away. Halfway there, one of Dean's sorority sisters (who seemed to multiply the older she got) invited us to stop at her home and freshen up. Passersby hugged Dean as if she were a member of

Willie's family. *Wasn't it a wonderful service? Yes, Willie was something. Oh, that Willie!* After they were gone, Dean asked her college friend if the strangers had mistaken her for someone.

"No," she replied. "They knew Willie loved you."

At the graveside service a bugler played "Taps" and another played echo from a nearby hill. Willie had performed the "Taps" duet many times, and so had I. This anthem of nightfall is so complete in its purpose, so perfect in its statement, that no bugler wants it to end.

V. Every Day by the Sun

- 36 -

I'M GOING TO HAVE TO WRITE THE DAMNED BOOK

AFTER WILLIE'S FUNERAL DEAN BEGAN TO HAVE TROUBLE breathing. The tightness in her chest was like nothing she'd ever experienced. Suspecting emphysema I took her to Dr. Shaun Helmhout, in Oxford, who put her through a series of tests. The diagnosis hit us like a sledge hammer. Dean had chronic obstructive pulmonary disease, a combination of chronic bronchitis and emphysema. COPD is progressive and incurable. As we left the clinic I searched for something positive to say.

"The disease is in the early stages," I began. "With medication and therapy—"

"It's a death sentence," Dean cut in. She clung to my arm. "Now I'm going to have to write the damned book!"

For a year and a half, sitting in a straight-backed chair with one foot twisted under her, Dean wrote in longhand nearly every morning. After lunch she'd take a nap while I typed what she'd written. She loved waking up to find her words waiting, stories she'd never told, stories bottled up since childhood. At night Nannie, Pappy, and Louise came to her in her dreams. *Write this, write that! Don't forget what I told you.* She'd turn on the bedside lamp and make notes in pencil.

"I'm like Ben Hur in search of his soul," she said, "except what I'm looking for isn't Christianity but *me*."

The memories she chose to write about were the signposts of her life. *Turn Here. Slow Down. Children Playing. Proceed with Caution.* With the pages of her life spread out before her she unraveled the riddle of Dean Faulkner Wells.

It was a story not without sadness but with an undeviating compass-heading of love and fidelity. A fatherless child was passed from one set of grandparents to the other. Until first grade she was unaware that she had no father. She had three uncles William, Jack, and John. She had a grandfather, "Papa" Hale. Her mother, Louise, gave her unstinting love. Her grandmothers Pearl Hale and Maud Falkner adored her. Estelle taught her social graces. William taught her to treasure the written word. And so she tackled a schoolmate who taunted, "You ain't got no daddy!" They fought until the teacher separated them.

That bicentennial July 4th in 1976 when she sailed above Oxford in "Miss Cotton," with the wind at her back and the morning sun in her face, she sensed her father's presence. And when she opened her father's pilot's license and saw his photo taken at age twenty-seven, she felt a physical connection with him.

"I'm going to call my book 'The Pilot's Daughter,'" she declared, clutching the pilot's license in her hand.

Looking back, while she might regret time wasted, things left undone, opportunities lost, mistakes made in haste, not knowing her place in the world or whether she was loved for herself or for her uncle's fame was no longer a concern. She finally knew what no one could teach her—though many had tried, myself among them—that she was neither a clone of her father nor the "second coming," nor a footnote to her uncle's achievement.

She was Dean.

Meanwhile, she'd wake at night unable to breathe, groping for a pill, her oxygen count so low she could have a stroke at any time. She made a pact with Death. *Let me finish the book, please sir, and then I will fly into the sun.* Sometimes I'd get her a glass of water. Other times she refused to wake me. My breathing was so regular, she told me, that she felt I was breathing for her.

"This anaconda is crushing the life out of me," she said one morning. Her oxygen level was depleted. She napped every two or three hours. I repeatedly tried to get her to use oxygen but she refused. "No tubes in my nose, thank you!"

"The trick to winning is not to give up," I said.

"You keep saying that," she replied, "but I'm starting to feel like Rip Van Winkle's great-great-granddaughter."

Her daily regimen began with eight medications including one for blood pressure and a painkiller. For ten minutes, she inhaled the steam of an electric vaporizer. She took a steroid, which like most serious medications had side-effects. She was supposed to stop taking it every two weeks to let her body recover.

"If steroids allow me to breathe," she insisted, "I will take them until the day I die!"

Sometimes she couldn't write fast enough, running out of legal pads and in her haste turning to backs of envelopes. Other times her mind would go blank.

"Why am I writing this book?" she demanded. "What do I know that matters?"

"Write the truth," said her typist. "You do that better than anyone."

Her remedy for writer's block was to work in the garden, read for pleasure, do the *New York Times* crossword, cook with wine, listen to music. With my typing duties temporarily halted, I resumed work on a novel that I'd put aside. Without telling me, she sat down and wrote the final chapter. I was working at my computer when she tiptoed up behind me.

"*It's done!*" she cried, surprising me. I was so startled that for a second or two I couldn't think of anything to say. "No congratulations?" she said, suddenly furious. "*You're fired!*" It was like that night at the Sizzler when she refused to ride home with me. I followed her to the kitchen and tried to apologize. Of course I was delighted that she'd finished and very pleased for her. "No, you need to work on your own stuff," she added. "I'll hire a typist."

"But we've come all this way—" I slumped on the kitchen bench. My left arm went numb, the sign of a heart attack.

"What's the matter?" she said.

I began hyperventilating. "Go urgent care."

"I'm not falling for that trick!" she said. I staggered into the hall while Dean, who ordinarily had trouble walking, followed with ease. "You can't go to the clinic dressed like that!" she said. I struggled to remove a pajama top. Standing on tiptoe, she pulled it off. We'd exchanged roles. She was the healthy one. It was all she could do to keep from laughing.

At the urgent care clinic my EKG test came back normal. I argued with the physician, saying I must have had a heart attack. Otherwise, why had my left arm gone numb? His response was a prescription for an anxiety medication. On the way out Dean offered me a steadying hand. "Why didn't you have a heart attack when I threatened to tear up our marriage license?" she said.

"Because you weren't writing a book then!" I said.

If our marriage was about anything it was finishing what we'd started.

One day not long after that, a motorcycle rumbled in the driveway. The rider raced the engine for good measure. Was this who we thought it was?

We went to the door and there stood Hannah, portable oxygen tank on his shoulder, plastic tubes up his nose. He entered the hallway where, in 1983, I had waltzed him out of the house. Now he embraced both of us, knocking our heads together.

"You are my people," he said, holding us in a stiff embrace, the silence broken only by the hum of his oxygen pump.

He'd come to say goodbye.

I made coffee for three. We sat in the kitchen. Hannah held the coffee cup in both hands and blew on it. His hands began to shake. He put down the cup. "You are givers. I'm a taker. I am unworthy."

"We give only a part of ourselves," Dean told him. "You give everything. *Geronimo Rex, Airships, Ray, Yonder Stands Your Orphan, Never Die.*"

He lit a cigarette. "Do y'all remember the time my wife threatened to shoot me?"

After the university hired Barry to teach creative writing, he celebrated by going on a two-week binge during which he met his future wife, Susan Avent, at the Hoka. Ronzo, town crier, reported to one and all that Hannah was in love.

Days later the Phantom pilot woke up in Arkansas and saw that Susan was wearing a wedding ring. Hannah claimed that his signature on the license was a forgery, the justice of the peace who married them was a charlatan, and that he barely knew this woman. Couldn't a man have a drink in peace?

"I shed wives like Hemingway," he told anyone who would listen.

Undeterred, Susan moved in, cleaned house, and sent for her children. Thus began their twenty-year war. They fought in their home, workplace, bars and restaurants. They rode to cocktail parties in separate vehicles. They called 911 so many times the police stopped coming. Hannah chronicled profane exchanges with Susan so often, so impishly, we wondered if he married her for material.

"Living the dream," he called it.

He never groped Dean again but did something which as far as Susan was concerned was far worse. He placed Dean on a pedestal. "*That scrappy Faulkner woman will eat your heart at breakfast!*" Susan had heard all she wanted about Dean's scrappiness.

On the evening in question Barry phoned us saying, "My wife wants to shoot me. Come quick."

"Just a minute," I said.

Dean got on the line. Had he called the police? Yes, but he had told them to wait until Dean Faulkner Wells got there.

"I'm on the way," she said.

When we arrived, the police were indeed standing in the yard. Dean walked past them like a one-woman SWAT team. I'd never seen her so sure of herself. Hannah was the very picture of abject gratitude.

I waited at the bedroom door while Dean went inside. Wraith-like and spectral in pink nightgown Susan sat in bed cradling a shotgun. To me she looked like Linda Blair in *The Exorcist.* I wouldn't have been surprised if she'd levitated.

Before Dean could take the gun away she had to climb down from her pedestal. Susan had written saying, "*I hate you for being an ideal I can never live up to.*" Dean wrote back that Barry had made up an unreal image of her and begged Susan not to put stock in anything he said.

"That's easy for you to say," Susan wrote back. "You don't have to live with him." But from then on, she and Dean were friends, at least on the surface.

Dean sat on the bed and gently pushed Susan's hair back from her forehead. "Please let Larry and me take you to the hospital," she said. For some reason Susan liked me. Maybe she viewed me as a fellow victim. We'd both married into literature.

"I haven't slept in two days," Susan groaned.

"At the hospital they'll give you something to help you sleep," Dean said. Little by little Susan relaxed her grip on the shotgun. "Where's your housecoat?"

"Nobody knows what I've been through—" Susan said, pointing at a bathrobe on a chair.

While Dean helped her put on the housecoat, I kicked the shotgun under the bed. Dean took her hand and led her outside. In the yard the police pretended not to be impressed. Hannah was laughing up his sleeve. The cops had accidentally let him have some fun.

"A mere twelve-gauge is nothing to this Faulkner woman!" he sang as Dean and Susan emerged from the house. In the glow of a streetlight I saw Susan's jaw muscles twitching. "Officers, stand

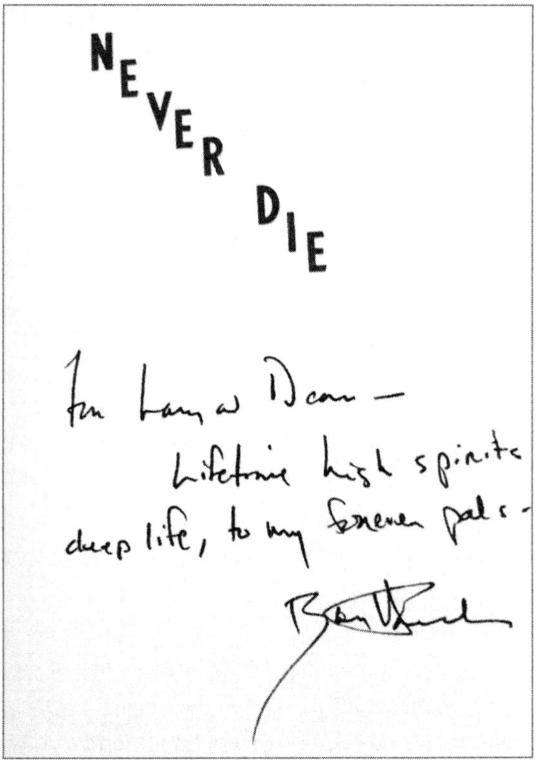

down," Hannah ordered. "My wife is no longer a danger to herself or others."

We laughed when he finished telling the story but all three of us felt like crying. He left us, oxygen tank still strapped to his shoulder, and roared away on his Harley.

On March 1, 2010, Barry Hannah died at home surrounded by his beloved dogs.

- 37 -

Every Day by the Sun

Crown Publishing Group released Dean's memoir in March of 2011 to coincide with her seventy-fifth birthday. A few days before the book launch I gave her a birthday party. The usual suspects came and toasted Dean and the forthcoming publication of *Every Day by the Sun*.

"I'm looking forward to your signing," Jack Pendarvis told her.

"Who will go in my place?" she demanded. Every writer in the room raised his or her hand.

"I've always wanted to be Dean," declared Pendarvis, who along with Lee Durkee, Wright Thompson, Ace Atkins, and Tom Franklin agreed to "impersonate" Dean at the signing.

"Seriously, each of you should read from *Every Day by the Sun*," I suggested. "Introduce yourselves as Dean Faulkner Wells and run with it."

Richard and Lisa Howorth staged the book launch at the Lyric Theatre. The turn-of-the-century building had been owned by Dean's great-grandfather, J. W. T. Falkner. It housed a livery stable operated by his son, Murry. William Faulkner and his brothers stabled their ponies there. Years later Oxford mayor Bob Williams converted the building to a movie theater. In 1932 *Today We Live*, the first movie adapted from Faulkner's work, premiered at the Lyric to be followed seventeen years later by *Intruder in the Dust*. At age thirteen, Dean attended that premiere with William, Estelle, Aunt Bama, Jill, and Vicki.

Where else but the Lyric should Dean's memoir have been released?

On the night of the signing the theater was filled to capacity. Jon, Diane, and Michael were there along with Dean's grandsons, Gus, Harry, and Keenan, who carried a bouquet of roses to give his grandmother. Dean nervously waited backstage as, one by one, Durkee, Atkins, Thompson, Pendarvis, and Franklin approached the microphone and declared, "My name is Dean Faulkner Wells."

"That man is an impostor!" Tom Franklin remarked of his predecessor. "*I'm* Dean Faulkner Wells." Each read a passage from the memoir until, finally, it was Dean's turn. I escorted her onstage. Due to medication and illness she was a bit unsteady as she leaned toward the microphone.

"I'm Dean," she said. The audience gave her a standing ovation that lasted two minutes. I couldn't have been prouder nor could I have loved her more than I did at that moment.

In his tribute to Dean, Wright Thompson recalled the electric atmosphere at the Lyric:

> We remembered her signing at the Lyric Theatre, where, as a little girl, she accompanied Pappy to the premiere of *Intruder in the Dust*. Crowds scared her, so she asked several local writers to read a segment before she talked at the end. We remember standing at the bottom of the stage, waiting to climb the steps through the curtain, and seeing Dean sitting on the ground, obviously about to melt down, and Larry next to her, holding her, calming her. They almost seemed like one person, and then, fortified, Dean walked out on stage and brought the house down. We'll never forget the feeling in that room—the way the town came out and seemed to realize that its emotional core lived inside of Deanie—and we'll never forget the even greater feeling hidden by the curtain, sitting on the ground near the foot of the stairs.

- 38 -

Wait

Take care of the dogs. Give them the treats they love. Water the plants. Make sure the children get each of the novels inscribed "To my girl Dean. Love, Pappy."

To move about the house she needed a walker. When she weeded the garden I sat beside her. "If you have a lustful feeling," I said, "even it's only a hot flash I'd like to be the first to know."

At the grocery she was determined to push the shopping cart. I followed like a proud father. On Friday we went to happy hour at City Grocery where I helped her up the stairs. After she got her breath back she blew kisses to waiting friends.

We didn't speak about the time we had left.

On July 24, 2011, she woke up complaining that her legs hurt. I thought of blood clots, but even a subject this serious couldn't be discussed until she'd had her morning coffee. The medications were to be taken with food. I fixed toast and asked if she wanted an egg. She wasn't hungry. I insisted that she eat something. She spread some cream cheese on a saltine cracker.

We'd been working on a new book entitled "Back Story," a collection of our magazine stories about Lake Placid, Key West, and San Francisco. I needed her to proofread her introduction. Work distracted her from the constant pain and anxiety. She sat at the kitchen table, one leg twisted underneath her as always, and made revisions in pencil. When she finished she went back to bed, saying she needed "a little nap." I took the revised pages and went to make her changes in the computer.

The written word which had brought us together was taking us to the last fork in the road.

Minutes later I went to check on her. She was lying in our brass bed, head propped up on pillows. I asked if I could get her anything. Without opening her eyes, she murmured, "Wait."

I went to my study and started to type the introduction. Then I realized what she'd said.

Wait? For what?

I hurried to the bedroom. She lay on her back, her eyes wide open, a smile frozen on her lips as if she were looking at someone she loved. She wasn't breathing. She had no pulse. I dialed 911 and requested an ambulance, then began doing CPR. That joyful smile terrified me. She looked thirty years younger. It was just like Dean to die smiling. I kissed her and told her that I loved her.

The ambulance arrived in total silence, no siren. I didn't realize the paramedics were at the door until they knocked. I let them in and they went to work, pumping Dean's chest so hard she bounced on the bed. It was painful to watch. Amazingly her smile never changed. It was as if she were in control while they, the paramedics, were going through the motions.

People don't die when they should but when they can.

The paramedics carried Dean to the ambulance where they restored a heartbeat using fibrillation. I phoned Jon and asked him to call his sisters.

At the hospital, a nurse in intensive care asked me if the patient had a living will. "Yes," I said. When Dean and her tennis partners were in their late forties they'd made an occasion of witnessing each other's living wills. They played two sets of doubles in ninety-degree heat, then went to lunch at the Downtown Grill and cosigned each other's living will.

"Let's go out in style!" they told each other.

I lost track of time as I waited in intensive care. Dean was brain-dead and being kept alive by a respirator until the children got there. Jon was the first to arrive. He went to his mother's bedside and teased her as though she could hear every word. How dare she leave without telling anyone where she was going? Paige, who had not seen her mother in a long time, looked diminished and vulnerable. I comforted her as best I could. Diane and Michael arrived along with their three sons. My daughter Catherine flew in from Ohio. Lawrence, my son, phoned from Prague offering to fly home. I thanked him and said that Dean would not expect him to come that far.

One by one Dean's friends greeted me at the hospital. Since only family members were allowed in intensive care they said goodbye to Dean through me. How many times had I done the same thing with spouses of dying friends? The waiting room filled up fast. As friends and acquaintances arrived, the reverent circle would shift and another respectful visitor would express regrets and ask about Dean's condition. Lisa Howorth brought a blanket and slept in the waiting room.

Connected by tubing to ventilator and monitoring machines, her face obscured by an oxygen mask, Dean slept. Electronic monitors beeped and glowed. Nurses and aides came and checked items off lists. The doctors arranged a meeting and asked the family's permission to take her off life support. To know that this was Dean's stated wish didn't make the decision any easier.

The children took their leave in the order in which they left for school. First Diane, then Paige and Jon, each pausing as if expecting a kiss and a lunch bag. Michael said goodbye to his mother-in-law and former tennis partner. I held her hand, felt her warmth, memorized the scent of her hair. Her artificially induced breathing sounded impatient as if she were eager to depart. We pretended she knew we were there. Then the nurses sent us out and closed the curtains.

We stood holding hands in the corridor, each thinking his own thoughts. Remember the good times, Dean told me before Willie's funeral. There was a night in Paris when she and I walked back to our hotel after dinner. A television set was playing in the lobby. I had a small bottle of cognac. As I looked for spare cups the rerun of a Spanish bullfight came on television. Without preamble, Dean began to call the bullfight like a sports announcer.

"See how the matador challenges the bull with his cape? That is called a *suerte de capote.*" I was aware that in 1956 Dean had toured Spain with Sandra Baker after attending the University of Geneva, but I had no idea that she knew so much about bullfighting. "The matador's suit of lights is custom-made," she went on. "It has silver or golden thread. It's called a *traje de luces.*" There in the Hotel Racine lobby watching a miniature black-and-white TV she poured out her admiration for bullfighters. "Watch the matador's feet! It's all about his feet. If he moves an inch, the crowd will turn on him. Watch his feet. If he moves he's a *coward.*" I stared not at the television but at my wife. If she believed in anything it was courage. That, I now realized, was Pappy's lesson in the lightning storm. Courage was her legacy. No wonder she died smiling.

The nurses opened the curtains. They had removed the oxygen mask and combed her hair, parting it in the middle and fanning it out as if a breeze had sprung up. Dean had never looked more beautiful.

She'd left funeral instructions inside her Betty Crocker cookbook. She wanted a no-frills graveside service like the one we'd given Louise.

At Oxford Memorial Cemetery as the pallbearers carried Dean's casket up the hill where family members and a hundred mourners waited, a string quartet composed of university music faculty members played her favorite passage from Vivaldi's *Four Seasons.* Jim Dees opened the graveside service reading a stanza from Wallace Stevens's "Sunday Morning." Then Jack Pendarvis read "Death Is Nothing at All" by Henry Scott Holland.

Death is nothing at all
I have only slipped away into the next room . . .

Lee Durkee read a short passage from St. Thomas More's letter to his daughter, which Dean heard at a Faux Faulkner judging party at Elaine's Restaurant in New York. She'd scribbled on a napkin:

Pray for me
And I shall for you and for all your friends
That we may merrily
Meet in Heaven.

Accompanied by guitar and bass the assembled mourners sang "Bye, Bye, Blackbird." The Reverend Taylor Moore gave a prayer of benediction.

Short and sweet.

At the wake friends and family crowded into the kitchen, where Diane and Catherine made sure everyone got enough to eat. Jon and Michael kept glasses filled.

After the well-wishers had left and the family had gone to bed, I checked the time. The electric clock on our bedside table had stopped at 10:35 a.m. It occurred to me that this was when she stopped breathing. The clock was running on Dean-time. Vowing never to buy another bedside clock I turned off the light and fell asleep.

Out of the darkness came Dean's smile, and the white Oldsmobile that had carried us to the Sizzler, and Willie standing beside it holding a bouquet of roses and Barry grinning from the backseat of eternity.

"*Don't get in the car!*" I mumbled in my sleep and Dean giggled as she did when I thought I was having a heart attack, her husky laughter tumbling across the divide.

I woke at dawn. I'd slept in my clothes. The house smelled like whiskey. Morning light blazing through the interior shutters cast a jagged shadow on the wall. I got out of bed and took a closer look. At the left side of the jagged-edged shadow I made out Dean's profile and on the right side of the shadow, etched in sunlight, the unmistakable, hawk-like silhouette of William Faulkner. *"Let me finish the book, please sir, and then I will fly into the sun."* Like her father Dean had lived every day by the sun. It was not surprising that sunlight was her final means of communication.

The marriage license! Had she carried out her threat to tear it up? Until then I hadn't had the nerve to look. I opened the chest of drawers where she kept our official documents. When was the fight at the Sizzler? Fifteen years ago? Twenty? I dug through silk scarves, bracelets, passports, photos. What had we fought about? Oh, yes, where Catherine would go to college. A sudden image of Dean marching along the shoulder of the highway paralyzed me. At the bottom of the bureau drawer I found family snapshots of Dean, her mother, and the children in their Sunday best. I was in one of the group photos. Louise must have taken it. The top of my head was cut off. Then I came upon an official-looking envelope. My hands shook as I broke the seal. I opened the document and recognized the date, October 6, 1972. Dean had rescheduled the ceremony so we wouldn't be married on my first wedding anniversary. I turned back to the wall to share my relief and gratitude, but in those few, precious seconds the sunlight had shifted and the shadow was gone.

THE END

Acknowledgments

With apologies to Cathie Pelletier's fans I'm deeply grateful to Cathie for delaying the writing of her twelfth novel to evaluate my manuscript. Her suggestions and encouragement were invaluable. Given her close friendship with Dean she also helped fill gaps in the story.

For sharing memories and/or photos I'd like to thank the University of Mississippi Archives and Special Collections, the *Commercial Appeal*, Sandra Baker Moore, Wright Thompson, David Rae Morris, Bruce Newman, Maude Clay, Murray Riss, Jim Dees, Susie James, Dianne Falkner, Alen MacWeeney, Chip Cooper, Kathy Ferguson, Vanessa Jones, Lena Jones, Hunter Cole, Lele Gillespie, John Morgan, Keith Gore Wiseman, Mara and Melanie Buffett, Glennray Tutor and, in memoriam, Ron Shapiro. Writers here in Oxford's literary community who know what it's like to labor in Faulkner's shadow gave steady support and reinforcement. I thank them for their candor and insight.

I'd like to thank my editor Craig Gill and Carlton McGrone at University Press of Mississippi, and copy-editor Deborah Upton.

Finally, for proofreading, encouragement, and inspiration I am forever indebted to Kathleen Wickham.

Index

About the Author

Lawrence Wells began his publishing career at Yoknapatawpha Press by editing the photo-biography *William Faulkner: The Cofield Collection*, by Jack Cofield. Author of two historical novels, *Rommel and the Rebel* and *Let the Band Play Dixie*, Wells received the 2014 Faulkner-Wisdom award for narrative nonfiction at the Words and Music Festival. He scripted an Emmy-winning 1994 Mississippi ETV documentary, *Return to the River*, narrated by James Earl Jones. His magazine articles have been distributed by the New York Times Syndicate.